Acting
The Australian Way

Acting
The Australian Way

Paul Parker (B.Ed.)
International Acting
Teacher/Acting Coach

Your Complete Guide to Becoming an Actor
Learn how to:

- Connect yourself with the text
- Enhance your breath and voice
- Explore and take risks
- Develop the inner you
- Empower yourself
- Be professional

And much, much more...

Edited by:

John Mapps. Sydney, Australia.

Typesetting by: Trisha Fuentes, California, USA.

Front and back cover design:

Hollie Kirby. Melbourne, Australia.

Images & Articles:

All images used in this book are either property of Paul Parker and his school AIDA, or have been used with permission of the copyright-holders, who are acknowledged in the captions. I thank all the organizations who have approved the use of their material in this book. All reasonable efforts were made to obtain permission to use copyright material, but if material has inadvertently been used without permission, the author welcomes information in this regard.

Publisher:

Self - Publishing with IngramSpark.

© Copyright:

Paul Parker, Melbourne, Victoria, Australia, 2022.

This book is dedicated to, and in loving memory of, actor **Reg Evans**. Reg was taken from us in the Black Saturday Bushfires in Australia on 7 February 2009.

Reg was an Australian (born in Wales, UK), an extraordinary actor of both comedy and drama, of both stage and screen. With a wealth of stage experience, from Melbourne and Queensland Theatre Companies to 83 IMDB film and television credits and numerous commercials.

My friend, my teacher and my life coach. Thank you Reg. I love and miss you. You were like a father to me.

About the author

As a teacher

Paul Parker is a qualified teacher with a Bachelor of Education in Drama, Literature and Language linguistics. He graduated from Deakin University/Victoria College – Rusden Campus in Melbourne, Australia, in 1991.

Paul began teaching *acting* in 1990 in Australia. He has also taught in the USA, Japan, China, South Korea and England.

Paul is the founder/Artistic Director/Head Lecturer/Teacher of AIDA - the Australian Institute of Dramatic Arts. He founded the school in June 2002 in Los Angeles.

Above: Paul Parker teaching his students' breath and voice in the AIDA school in Hollywood in 2008

As a judge / adjudicator

USA – *on screen*

Paul was one of the entertainment industry judges, including prominent Los Angeles Casting Directors, Agents & Managers, that were judging actors work on screen, for IPAC - International Performing Arts Conference in Los Angeles, USA, from 2007 to 2010. Paul also opened these four conferences with a one hour acting class, to an audience of over a thousand people.

AUSTRALIA – *on stage*

Paul was the adjudicator at the One Act Play Festival in Ararat, Victoria in 2014.

Picture above: Paul adjudicating the One Act Play festival in Ararat in 2014. Picture courtesy of the Ararat Advertiser newspaper, Australia.

As a director

Paul began his work as a Director in 1990 in Melbourne. He has also directed in Japan and in the USA.

As of early 2022, Paul had directed twenty-seven theatre productions and seven short films. As well as various show reels for students. He has also worked as an assistant director at the highest level in Australian theatre.

As this book goes to print, Paul is in post-production on his 7th short film and in an advanced stage of script development on his first feature film.

Above: The third AIDA Showcase playbill. This show performed and toured Hollywood in Los Angeles, San Francisco and Off Broadway in New York in 2009. Students performing include Gerald Webb, a student for more than two years, who has 95 IMDB credits as of June, 2022, as well as Cyanne McClairian (a seven times award-winning stage actor), Lauren Simon, Adam Jennings, Kaleena Massaker, Pam Poulson, Sam Aaron, Tara Lyn Joseph and Melody Mathews.

As an actor

Paul began acting in high school in Melbourne in 1975, and first performed stand-up comedy in 1977.

Paul worked as a professional actor in Australia and then later in the USA from 1979 to 2003.

He has won two acting awards.

For more details, please see the full curriculum vitae at the back of this book or go to the following websites:
www.aidaacting.com
www.paulparkerpc.com.au
www.player-productions.com
Or Paul's IMDB page:
https://www.imdb.com/name/nm1296339/?ref_=fn_al_nm_2

Above: We couldn't find the original, but we found a photocopy. The Australian television paper TV Week, in the week of 18 August 1979. Main photo: Paul Parker, fourth in line behind Richard Morgan, Steven Tandy and Norman Yemm. Bottom right picture: Paul, left front of the cart, with Richard Morgan and Steven Tandy.

Paul wishes to thank Are Media Pty Limited/Are Media AU Publication /TV Week from August 18th, 1979. Approved by Rhiannon Hedges. Syndication Lead. Syndication & Digital Library, Content Services, Photography & Syndication. Are Media. Level 1. 54 Park Street, Sydney, NSW 2000.

> **The Beverly Hills/Hollywood NAACP**
> Twelfth Annual Theatre Awards
> presents
>
> # P.J. Parker
> with
> **Certificate of Nomination**
> for
> *Ensemble*
>
> *For the Love of Freedom: Part I Toussaint*
>
> **Local**
>
> _____   _____
> President   Awards Chairperson
>   November 12, 2001

USA – ACTING AWARD

Above: the nomination for the award.

Please note: while living in the USA, Paul Parker changed his name to PJ Parker; as there was already a person named Paul Parker in the Screen Actors Guild.

Above: Paul won Best Actor in an Ensemble Cast for The Love of Freedom at the NAACP Awards. Pictured above with Director Ben Guillory from Robey Theatre Company at the Directors Guild on Sunset Boulevard in Los Angeles in 2001. Paul wishes to thank Ben Guillory & Danny Glover at Robey Theatre Company for giving permission to put this picture in the book.

AUSTRALIA - ACTING AWARD

*Above: **Best Actor Winner** – of a heat & **Runner Up to best Actor** - of a heat, in a television role, where Paul was given a prize amount of money at Ballarat South St., Eisteddfod, Australia, 1998.*

This judge sheet above appears with thanks to Australian Casting Director icon Jan Russ.

10514 Forbes Avenue, Granada Hills, CA 91344

Talking Theatre
with Don Grigware
July 13, 2001 - July 26, 2001

Funnyman Charles Nelson Reilly is treading the boards once again! "Save It for the Stage", his one man "longest show in town", staged by Paul Linke, is now playing at the El Portal Mainstage Theatre. At the Falcon last summer, the show came in at three and one-half hours and now it maybe runs a few minutes shorter. Audiences buy it, because they love Charles so much. He laughs at himself as do all great clowns and finds humor in the saddest of circumstances. When he talks about his mother, Uncle Benny, Aunt Lillian and his Swedish grandparents in Hartford and their nightly toss of herring bones from the dinner table across the room into the toilet, he reduces you to tears.

The evening is singular and wonderful, but please, Charles, cut off some more time! Love ya!...Speaking of veteran performers, the adorable Debbie Reynolds did one night at the Alex in Glendale on June 16 for VHA Home Care and was nothing short of sensational. At 69, she's still a beauty, can still sing with the best of them and her incredible impression of Zsa Zsa can only be topped by her turn as "superstar" GS...The Greenway Arts Alliance and the Robey Theatre Company are now presenting the very ambitious project "For the Love of Freedom; Part One: Toussaint (The Soul) Rise and Revolution" by Levy Lee Simon and directed by Ben Guillory at the Greenway Court Theatre in Hollywood-some spectacular staging is accomplished here by Mr. Guillory and the marvelous acting ensemble headed by M. Darnell Suttles as Toussaint L'Ouverture is top-notch. P.J. Parker is a standout as the evil Sonthonax.

The story of Haiti is fascinating and deserves to be told. Four terrific ladies begin the story as a chorus, much like in the great 70's hit "For Colored Girls Who Have Considered Suicide When the Rainbow is Enough" and they are a joy to behold, as are many of the scenes, but at almost four hours in length, much pruning and editing is necessary. Great praise goes to Tom Meleck for his unbelievable set design, to Naia Akacem-Sanders for her elegant costumes and hair and to choreographers Carol Bristol and Yvans Jourdain.

Since the action is played out on stages surrounding the audience, it is fun to watch, but the constant playing of the drums is distracting and makes some actors inaudible..."House" by Tom McCormack is making its premiere at the Falcon Theatre, about the inner workings of a publishing company. As the cold, ruthless mogul Ted, Harry Hamlin is perfection and heads a very solid cast. William Schallert has never been better. Neil Vipond tugs at the heartstrings as an aging employee mishandled by the firm. Tom McCormack created and ran St. Martin's Press for many years and makes a bold statement about cutthroat business tactics vs. artistic integrity...Finishing up its run at the Black Dahlia Theatre is Austin Pendleton's savory "Orson's Shadow" (see my list of award picks), directed with precision by Matt Shakman.

Brilliant characterizations from Robert Machray as Orson Welles and Jeff Sugarman as Laurence Olivier make this a must-see. Pendleton has a keen eye for the foibles of his leading men and their struggles are portrayed eloquently...Expert is the only way to describe the acting ensemble at Actors Alley and their sheer professionalism adds much to the very dated and wornout "A Thurber Carnival". Gwen Van Dam and Stuart Thompson are outstanding in one of a few enjoyable sketches titled "The Macbeth Murder Mystery"...Lisa Mordente, daughter of Chita Rivera and her songwriting hubbie Donnie Kehr recently did a concert staging of "Pandora's Box" at the El Portal Mainstage.

This project of Kehr's has been in the producing stages for a few years and has potential. Currently, the story and characters need more fleshing out, as the concert book reads more like an outline than a finished product.

Some great songs permeate the hourlong tale and terrific performances came from diva Michele Meis, Zaxariades, Christina Souza, Jason Martinez and Paul Leighton, also producer. Great choreography as well from Barry Lather...Until next time...

Above: The last sentence of the second paragraph reads. "PJ Parker is a standout as the evil Sonthonax" in Robey Theatre's play For The Love of Freedom in Hollywood, in 2001.

Paul wishes to thank the newspaper "Valley Scene" for the approval of this play review going into the book. Approved by Trisch Kushner. Valley Scene Magazine. 6520 Platt Avenue Suite 336. West Hills, CA 91307. USA

Presents

The "James Boag" Actors

in

The AIDA Revue

Above: The first ever AIDA Acting School Showcase playbill cover. Directed by Paul Parker in Hollywood in 2004.

Contents

Foreword 15
Introduction 21
Prologue 25

Part 1
Theory 29

Chapter 1 About actors and acting 31
Chapter 2 What helps actors stand out from other actors? 39
Chapter 3 Teaching: Theory and practice 45
Chapter 4 Training the actor: Introducing Australian techniques 67
Chapter 5 International theorists: Four other techniques that I teach . 113
Chapter 6 Preparing for an audition 127
Chapter 7 Improvisation 145
Chapter 8 Making the right decisions: Student case studies 153
Chapter 9 Training the experienced actor 181

Part 2
Practice 187

Chapter 10 Having the right attitude 189
Chapter 11 Acting on stage 195
Chapter 12 Australian techniques: Dropping In The Text 203
Chapter 13 You 221

Appendix 1 Handouts 237
Appendix 2 Lesson plans 251
Appendix 3 People who influenced my teachings 255
Appendix 4 The AIDA school and successful students 257
Appendix 5 Paul Parker full curriculum vitae as teacher/coach 263

Above: Paul at the 2011 Academy Awards.

Below: Paul with Jean Gillmore, 2006 Academy Awards.

Both pictures taken at the Kodak Theatre, Hollywood. Los Angeles. All Academy Awards photos were approved to appear in the book in January 2022, by Kristen Ray - Senior Specialist, Clearance. Academy of Motion Picture Arts and Sciences.
8949 Wilshire Blvd. Beverly Hills. CA 90211

Foreword – with American actress and Casting Director Nicole Dionne

Paul Parker and I met in the early 2000. My talent manager at the time, who was Australian, got word about this great Australian acting teacher in Los Angeles and suggested I go check out his class.

Paul's Australian techniques and breath work really resonated with me. Coming freshly off a dance degree, I was very in tune with my body and tapping into emotions. The chakra and breathing exercises took my emotional connection to another spiritual level. I was too young and green at the time to realize it, but looking back, my acting life also became a healing journey.

Paul's auditioning and on-camera classes were really where I excelled and learned things I had never heard of before. Paul's classes were pivotal for me in understanding camera angles, my best angles, framing, the pacing of a set, 'less is more' acting on camera, and how to draw your audience in with your eyes. He gave me tricks to stay connected take after take. He showed me the importance of really listening in order to respond to my scene partner authentically. Paul would play back our performances and give us positive feedback and constructive criticism. Each note you get from Paul is very specific to you.

Paul as a teacher is definitely intuitive and maybe a bit of an Empath. Not just with his students acting, but with their personal insecurities, hang ups, self-doubts, unhealthy relationships, distractions and anything else he can sense you are struggling with. Fact is, most of us have something is our lives that can throw us off our game or bad habits we create to sabotage ourselves from success. I love that Paul is the kind of teacher who isn't afraid to help you look at yourself deeper. This is a good teacher, a teacher who cares enough to tell you the truth, even if it's hard to hear, even if they have to deal with a "shoot the messenger" reaction from their student. Teachers like Paul go that extra mile in hopes that they can get you out of your own way so you can succeed.

So, what makes me an expert on why you should read this book, and believe in Paul's teachings? Well, I have put most of this information in practice myself. And I am a constant curious student of life. At this point I can say I have built up quite a lot of experience in making mistakes, having regrets, creating wins, experiencing miracles, surviving heart break, being the glue that connects people, shifting and pivoting my dreams, starting a business, and making it in this town this long without quitting all together. I have been in this business for almost twenty-one years now, and I still feel like I have more to learn, but I am also very savvy at this point to know what works.

I learned so much in my years with Paul and private coaching for auditions that I was already able to use it fully in the real world of acting. Breaking down my scripts into beats, creating intentions, finding surprises, taking risks, all those nuances I learned to add to my prep work, never left me. I had such a great time attracting roles that quite literally gave me an outlet to heal and work through my emotional scars.

The most interesting thing about reconnecting to Paul now after so many years is my new awareness about how much he enriched and influenced who I am in this industry and how I operate as a casting director as well as an actor. I almost couldn't believe I was still using the skills Paul taught me in acting class for my casting career today.

When I watch auditions coming in from actors, I ask myself these questions:

Is this person right for this role?

Do I believe what they are saying?

Are they listening when they aren't speaking?

Do they feel grounded and confident in their performance and slate?

Are they off book and dropped into their text?

Are they taking risks or finding interesting surprises in the script that others aren't catching?

Do I want to keep watching them or am I over it in twenty seconds?

Did they commit to their choices?

Do I want to bring them back for another role, even if this one isn't quite right for them?

The list goes on. But I think you get the idea.

Reading Paul's book brought back so many memories and moments of nostalgia for me but it was also a great reminder of how far I have come and how much I have learned along the way, not just in my acting but in how I lead and support my life.

Who knew the breath and chakra work would lead me to loving Yoga, specifically Kundalini Yoga? Who knew breaking down a script and analyzing dialogue would lead to me writing my own scripts? Who knew that finding subtext in a scene would help me navigate what other's words really mean in business and relationships? Who knew that it would give me a keen eye into how best to cast our movies?

This book covers so much ground from practical exercises to personal development, that it's probably not for the "I just want to get rich and famous" quick crowd. This is for the Artist. This is for *the actor*, of course, but there are so many helpful chapters in here that I feel would be beneficial insight for singers, singer-songwriters, visual artists, dancers, public speakers and leaders of different industries.

These chapters aren't just about technique, methods, and tricks of the trade, Paul also brilliantly calls out issues of the human artist's condition. He speaks to things like having self-awareness about our strengths and weaknesses, and how to navigate through those dualities. He speaks to more complex topics like co-dependency, abuse, and mental illness, which are ever-present in our creative communities. These are very important issues in any field, but especially in the entertainment industry, and I am so grateful he is shining a light on them here in this book.

I wish I had a book like this before I moved to Hollywood. I just happened to be one of the lucky ones that got to meet Paul very early on in my career, and to get a chance to be exposed to this kind of thinking. This book, in my mind, would be a great addition to a curriculum for the colleges of Performing Arts. And I plan to suggest it to my old theater professors.

Whatever you choose to pursue in this business, chances are it's calling your soul. Paul's personal path and his teachings have such a wide range of in-depth information and exercises to help you on your own journey. How you evolve over the years in this kind of career is a bit of a mystery and so personal to every individual.

Acting is one of those careers that do not have a guaranteed map to success, it's a bit closer to searching for hidden treasure from a napkin drawing. But you do have choices you will make and actions you will take to get to your goals. Best if you do all that prepared and trusting yourself, so you can confidently move forward, fearlessly. And when you get there, you'll be pleasantly surprised with how easy it is to book the work!

All I can say for sure is, if you connect with what is laid out in this book and you do the work, you are giving yourself a strong foundation for success, one way or another. If you decide you like Paul's teaching enough to train or be coached by him, then I can say from personal experience that you will be in good hands. He is one of those teachers who truly care about his student's fulfillment in their careers, while having a healthy life. He is in it for your success. He is in it for your personal growth. He is in it to create a community that supports each other through wins and losses. And I have to say; I do miss being a part of that.

Good luck wherever this acting journey takes you. Maybe I will see your audition tape for one of my movies one day. Or maybe you'll hire me to cast one of your own films! My wish for all of you artists reading this is that you believe in your worthiness and that all your dreams come true.

Paul, thank you for sharing all that you do with the world. I am touched and humbled that you would ask me to be one of the first eyes to read this rich and insightful book and even more honored that you would trust my words for your introduction. I love you and am forever grateful for who you have been in my life.

So without further ado...enjoy the lessons and trust the process. Your actor self will thank you.

Nicole Dionne

Nicole has 44 IMDB credits as an actor and 40 IMDB credits as a Casting Director/ Casting Department at Stella Nova Casting, as of June, 2022

Introduction

The Australian actor training in this book will make you a better actor and help you achieve your acting goals.

The book is divided into two main parts: Part 1 Theory, and Part 2 Practice. The Theory section talks about a way to live your life as an actor as well as teaching you Australian Techniques. The Practice section gives you tangible exercises to do as well as giving you information on how and why to do these things.

As well as acting theory and practice, you will read a bit about me and my journey as an actor and teacher. I also give many examples and scenarios from students I have taught because we can often learn from other people's mistakes and by discussing different ways of doing things.

You will learn about connecting with the text and with the importance of breath and voice. You will learn about risk-taking, developing the inner you, along with many other subjects from my school's curriculum. With the theory and practice and case studies, this book is your working guide on acting training.

I teach five acting techniques as well as movement and mask exercises from Frenchman Jacques Lecoq. All five of the techniques will be mentioned in the book, with the focus on Australian techniques. The five acting techniques are:

- Australian techniques
- Polish technique – Jerry Grotowski
- Hungarian technique – Rudolph Laban
- Russian technique – Constantin Stanislavski
- German technique – Bertolt Brecht (an approach to performing his work)

This book is aimed at actors of all levels, beginners, intermediate and advanced. "Every day's a school day", Rotarian, Walter S. Young first said in 1921 in the USA, hence I believe that actors at all levels will receive benefit from this book.

For example, you will discover:

- how the mind and body work
- a better way to think and behave
- ways to eliminate bad habits or blockages
- a sense of unspoken camaraderie, as actors think what happens to them only happens to them
- new acting techniques
- new acting skills and tips
- how to focus more professionally on your work
- inside knowledge and hypotheses from someone who has lived in the Australian and American entertainment industry markets for a long time

Who am I to write a book on the craft of acting? Who am I to say, *do this and do that*? Who am I to offer an alternative to other people's views or opinions? Or question their decisions? Who am I to say powerful things about Australian acting training? Well, all I can really do is, to humbly ask you, to read and consider what I write.

While putting the final touches to this book, one of my two sons called out while he was playing and being looked after by family. *Playing!* My son was playing. How important is playing for an actor?

As we begin this book, we will discuss, propose, coach, educate and empower one another. Yes, *we*. Not I. You see, as you read, you will think, you will grow. Hence, we will share this journey together.

Americans, please excuse me, but I have chosen to use British/Australian spellings (for example, theatre) and expressions (for example, acting teacher instead of acting coach).

For the most part I have also used "he" when discussing someone. Ladies, please just assume I mean "she" as well.

Finally, I would like to paraphrase the first words Sir Laurence Olivier said when he accepted his *Lifetime Achievement Award* for acting at the Academy Awards in 1979.

As he walked out in front of the cameras and the worldwide audience, he said, "Fellow students". And now let's begin.

Above: Paul attending the 59th Annual Golden Globes in 2002. The Golden Globes Awards picture above has been authorised to appear in print by Gregory P. Goeckner, COO and General Counsel, Hollywood Foreign Press Association, January 20th, 2022.

Above: Paul at the 2001 Academy Awards at Shrine Auditorium in Los Angeles.

Prologue

I am a lucky man. I have attended six Academy Awards ceremonies and two Golden Globes in the USA.

Here is a diary note from my 2011 Oscar awards experience.

On Sunday, February 27th, 2011, I drove with my friend Jean Gillmore (an industry animator who has been involved in the drawing of many famous characters in animated feature films) from my Hollywood apartment up Wilcox Avenue and along the Hollywood Boulevard en route to the Academy Awards.

We soon arrived at the Kodak Theatre and after a vehicle search, and a security check, we walked down the red carpet in front of all the lights and the media and the cameras.

Colin Firth was to our right, Gwyneth Paltrow to our left. Annette Bening and Warren Beatty were in front of us being interviewed. Halle Berry and Justin Timberlake were suddenly just next to us.

Above: At the 2011 Academy Awards at the Kodak Theatre. Here Paul is outside on Hollywood Boulevard in front of El Capitan Theatre.

Later, having drinks with industry people inside the Kodak Theatre, a very well-known television actor, William Wintersole, asked me for my business card, saying, "He knew some actors who needed a good acting coach".

As we left that evening, we took photos in front of Oscar statues, right next to Scarlett Johansson and Matthew McConaughey. As we walked away, off the red carpet, the winning actors from a previous year's awards, from the film *Slumdog Millionaire,* walked past us; as did other celebrities.

We were here – the Academy Awards! This was the sixth time for me. It was, as it always is, surreal, exciting, pretentious, fun and an amazing night for me, my friend and for all the film entertainment industry.

I have added this account because, for many, this is the realisation of an actor's dreams. Being at, or more importantly, being nominated at the Academy Awards in Hollywood! Is that your dream?

Above top: Paul at the Beverly Hilton Hotel and the Golden Globes with Sven, the President of the Hollywood Foreign Press, and his companion in 2002; and the late and great Aussie actor James Armstrong. The top picture has been authorised to appear in print by Gregory P. Goeckner, COO and General Counsel, Hollywood Foreign Press Association, January 20th, 2022.
Above below: A sample of what you receive when invited to the Academy Awards, including the tickets.

Above: Paul in rehearsal, playing Hamlet, in 2B Or Not 2B @ 2033. *An adaptation of Shakespeare's* Hamlet. *James Avery (180 IMDB credits) played Polonius in the production and is seated behind Paul, at the 2nd Stage Theatre, 6500 Santa Monica Blvd., Hollywood, Los Angeles. The play was directed by Tony Armatrading from the Royal Shakespeare Company/National Theatre in London. Below: a picture of the playbill from 2002.*

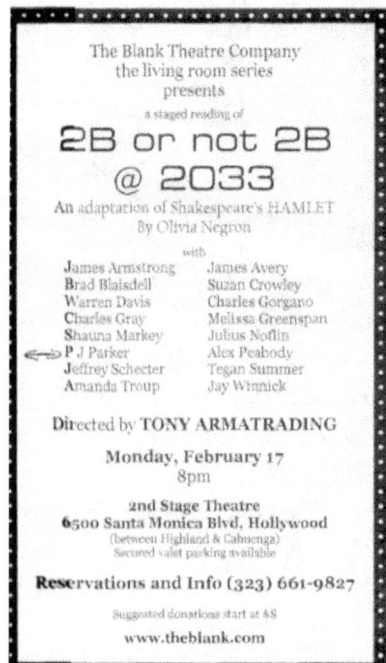

Part 1
Theory

Chapter 1
About actors and acting

At a class I taught in Hollywood, continuing my usual habit, I greeted with a hug all the actors as they arrived at class, and then complimented them.

Complimented them about their appearance or attitude or their talent. Or, in some other way, supporting their journey or achievements in their day.

During the course of the evening class, I gave all the actors only positive or constructive feedback about their work.

I laughed and joked with them, discussed stories with them and subtly gave them advice and taught them acting skills from lesson plans I had created. Lesson plans that had objectives for the students to achieve.

I also reminded the students of what we were working on that month in the camera class. As well as the specific goals that *they chose* and put down in their note books: the things that they wanted to work on that month.

We all learn best with positive reinforcement

One forty-year-old actor, who was three times her current size a couple of years ago, I complimented a lot. When she sat down in front of the camera, I said, "*G'day pretty lady*". She smiled, from ear to ear. She smiled for about one minute. That night she did the best work in class that she had done for many months.

In fact, all the actors did very well that night. Without sounding smug, we all know the answer why, don't we? Positive reinforcement. Open, friendly, candid, honest, encouraging and subtly empowering support was given to her, given to them all: the professional actors.

This is common behaviour for me in my teachings through my international teaching school, AIDA – Australian Institute of Dramatic Arts.

I should also say, I'm not always this sweet. I am extremely honest and direct at times, but I always come from a place of love with my constructive criticism.

This part of the book is about acting theory. Let's begin with a question and a definition.

What is an actor?

Actors are often a self-conscious and sometimes insecure bunch (I know I was one), and if you ask actors *why* they want to be an actor, sometimes they are not sure why.

I sometimes ask actors, "What is an actor?" They often will give me some reason as to *why* they are acting instead of a definition of what an actor actually is.

Some actors articulate that they like to personify the great characters written by great playwrights. Such as: Mother Courage from the play, *Mother Courage and Her Children* by Bertolt Brecht, or Blanche from *A Street Car Named Desire* by Tennessee Williams, or Lenny from *The Homecoming* by Harold Pinter, or Hamlet from *Hamlet* by William Shakespeare. But not *that many* say that.

Now I'm not here to talk down to anyone or assume anyone is at a certain level of intellect; so, I will just simply state what *I think* an actor is.

I believe an actor is someone who displays the human condition well. We, the audience, experience compassion, empathy, interest and understanding for a character's journey in the story that is being told. For example: we see a character's vulnerability. In support of this, we are emotionally moved by, you guessed it, the actor's performance. Ideally, we are not thinking of the actor, we're thinking of the character and the story that is unfolding for us.

Why act?

Why would you put yourself in the position where somebody else has to make the decision as to whether you work professionally or not? Why would you put yourself in the position where somebody else makes the decision (at a casting session) on whether or not you get money to pay your rent?

Some people might even ask: Why would you put yourself in the position where you depend on acceptance from others?

Now, I'm not going to talk too much about whether you should act or not, or whether you should wait for someone else to employ you or not. Simply because you will make your own decisions.

But I want you to know this entertainment industry statement that many people have said. I am not sure who said it first, but here it is, "If there's anything else you can do or anything else you want to do, as opposed to acting, you should do that".

Why would entertainment industry people say such a thing? Why is it a well-known saying in the acting business? It certainly is in both Australia and the USA.

Maybe it's because acting at the highest level takes courage, strength, intelligence, self-awareness, often self-development, creativity, skill, perseverance, practice, trust, an ability to play, as well as an ability to show vulnerability, use your imagination and take risks. You must have all this and some luck as you personify the human condition. The journey, most often, also needs guidance.

Unfortunately, not all aspiring actors will get to work professionally. Sad but true.

I am guessing that if you have bought this book, you are curious as to the successes of Australian actors and you want to know how they are trained.

Okay then. You have decided to be an actor. Good for you. So, let's get you trained the Australian way. *If* the Australian way works for you. If not, try another way. Because in the end, it is all about what techniques work best for you to help you get professional work.

I should state from the outset that acting and acting training have changed. Standing there and simply saying the lines with attitude, à la John Wayne fifty or sixty years ago, does not work anymore. An audience demands so much more from its actors in the 21st century.

I feel that I have to say this: generally speaking, especially in television, some actors get work based on their looks, their bodies, their charisma and/or their attitude; more so than the level of their talent. Usually, though, most of those actors do not last too long once their looks start to fade. Unless they have developed the skills to act well.

You might now be thinking: "Ah yeah, I can think of actors who I used to see on television a lot, but I don't see them in film". Or, if they did do a film: "Ah yeah, they did a film, they weren't that good and I haven't seen them that much after that".

One reason for this could be that behind their good looks and body, there was an inability to show the *human condition,* the nuances of human behaviour, very well.

Audiences nowadays can't stand seeing the actor acting. Audiences today want to see the nuances of human behaviour – real emotion, such as someone on the verge of tears, or tears rolling down a face, blushing, a nervous twitch, a repetitious action – all as a part of a character. They want to see truth. Or, what looks like the truth.

Developing acting skills requires intelligence. Intelligence from the actor to acknowledge this fact, humility to be able to adjust, and the desire to *learn skills* so they are able to progress and have a successful acting career.

I often say to actors, every male actor can act *arrogant* or play *an arsehole* and every female actor can act *bitchy*; but what else can you produce?

You should definitely ask yourself, "Why do I act? Why do I want to be an actor?"

Passion

In 1990, I worked with a large group of teenagers at a youth theatre company called St. Martins Theatre, in Melbourne, Australia.

It became apparent to me, very quickly, that there were *different* types and levels of four attributes of the students:

- commitment
- talent
- professionalism
- passion

All of these attributes are important to have. Passion, for example, is very important. One thing that people say to me and have said to me since I was very young, is that I am a very passionate person.

When I worked as an actor, and now as a teacher/coach/director – and probably in anything else that I have done or still do – I am always passionate.

Unfortunately, I see and coach some actors who don't have enough *passion* to make it as a professional actor. Hopefully this book will help encourage those people.

Acting is a tough profession. Especially financially. If one decides to be an actor, like I did for twenty-five years, let's hope that *you* commit to it one hundred percent and let's also hope that you are passionate.

Because, for many, it could be a long, hard, challenging road ahead. For many, believe it or not, it is a road of self-discovery and even self-development. In some ways, it was for me. Let's recall the question I asked earlier: *Why be an actor?* Because, sure, we can decide to be one. But, well, now please think, *why do I want to be an actor?*

Because this will influence your journey. If you just want to be an actor to obtain acceptance or love, you may not make it. If you just want to be an actor to become a celebrity, you may not make it. If you just want to be an actor to say, "See Mum, I told you I could do it!", you may not make it either.

Of course I hope this book helps guide you, educate you and provoke you into helping you achieve your goals as an actor.

Let's also hope that you have your mind set right too. I will elaborate on all of these points later in this book, but as you read on please have in mind the need for passion to act and the commitment to work hard and be professional at being an actor. Experienced actors, please read on also, and continue to work on your skills and learn new things.

Significance of repetitive language

My writings, thoughts and experiences are all naturally influenced by the fact that, as well as drama, I studied English literature and language linguistics for four years at University.

For example, at times during the course of this book I will generalise. I will utter a cliché or mention a stereotype. This is because I believe that there is validity in generalisations, clichés and stereotypes. If there wasn't, these words wouldn't still exist in our vocabularies.

However, even though I will utter generalisations, clichés and stereotypes to make a point, I will often counter-think. I will often look at the flip side, as I try to fully explain and stretch out some of my advice. I will do this to make it easier for you to understand the points I am making, and so we are both clear about what is being said.

Another reason I will do this is because, in my experience, many teachers, or people who call themselves teachers, constantly utter clichés or make comments and generalisations as they teach; and they don't explain fully what they mean. They just keep talking.

Such an approach leaves students confused: they will be left to dissect or not dissect, understand or not understand, agree or disagree, sink or swim. I will not do that.

I believe that everybody has the ability to act. The performer comes out in us all in many different ways.

For example, the traffic cop conducting traffic when the lights go out at a road intersection. There is a sense of performance in his orchestration. The lawyer in a courtroom who performs confidently for her client. And have you ever noticed somebody telling a story to another person? The scene is then noticed by a stranger, and then, when the story-teller notices that they're being watched by the stranger, they become more animated and enjoy the experience even more. They enjoy *being watched* as they tell the story. They're performing.

I see this often. You are at a bar and you see people arguing. They become even more animated as they notice that they are being watched, and get a sense of enjoyment from being watched. You guessed it. They're performing too.

What a resilient person you are. Pat yourself on the back. You are a working actor or an actor in training to be a professional one. You work as a barman, a waiter, in retail, you do after-school teaching programs, anything to help you pay the bills; well done. Be proud of your life. Be proud of your occupational *risk-taking* to want to achieve your goals and dreams of working as a professional actor or getting better as a professional actor. "Go get 'em!" I like to say.

Learning Point Number One

- Why are you an actor?
- Are you choosing to be an actor for the right reasons?
- Be passionate and professional and have strong commitment.
- Consider that part of your journey is one of passion, self-discovery and perhaps even self-development.

Chapter 2
What helps actors stand out from other actors?

Over my years in the entertainment business, dating back to 1977, the actor who *comes across* as confident when interacting with other people, and/or knows what they are doing, or looks like they know what they are doing, is the actor most likely to *make it*.

Whether they are internally confident, or faking it, or hiding their real thoughts or fears or not, is not that important. This is true even at the start of a person's acting journey.

Given their ability to *appear confident* on the surface – in meetings, in castings, on set – these people are more likely to book professional work or work more in the future.

The cliché *fake it till you make it* seems apt here. Because we're acting anyway, right?

An aside: I am being a bit tongue in cheek here because I do believe in real self-development, real acting training, including technique. I also do believe that it is more important in the long run for you to develop your *inner* self-confidence so you can act confidently.

With learning *how* to *act* confidently as your ultimate goal, your ongoing and long-term process should be an internal process and not an external one. That's because having inner confidence and belief is obviously better than *faking it till you make it*. It is much more profound because it is rooted in substance. Your substance.

But while you are working on your inner self-confidence, put on a brave *acted* face and body language and try to appear confident to help you in the meantime.

How to get internal self-confidence

Actors develop internal self-confidence by being paid to work as an actor and also because they work on building the strength and confidence from within them. A good teacher does the same with a student. I have seen and taught many hundreds of actors who have worked this way and had success.

For example, I suggest you:

- present yourself in a confident, positive way
- bring your true personality out in an as many circumstances as possible
- have acting training
- work on *you* by doing some self-development

Actors who do this usually then:

- start to book acting work
- build their career
- work with the best writers, directors, editors, lighting and set designers, etc.

So, consider working on the inner you to develop inner self-confidence, and in turn this will help you stand out from other actors.

What is the inner you?

The inner you

I believe the inner you is:

- an understanding of who you are
- why you are who you are
- why you think about who you are
- what you do
- how you do it
- how you react to certain circumstances
- your emotional capacities and capabilities

Many actors go into the acting profession because they want acceptance and love. In short, many go into the profession with issues. Now in my thirty-third year of teaching, as of 2022, actors have told me some very personal things about themselves. Things they need to accept. Things they need to heal. Things they need to deal with and get over.

I love actors, obviously I'm biased, but I think actors are extremely resilient. Not only do they develop the art to portray the human condition, but they also develop many other skills to help them pay their bills.

From all my experiences and teachings, I profoundly believe that the better you understand yourself and the way you think and live your life, the more empathy you will have with the characters that you create and audition and perform. The characters you create will be more detailed characters.

Working and developing your skills as an actor – in particular, being able to draw on emotions such as sadness, guilt, jealousy, anger and insecurity – cannot but help you get in tune with yourself or get you thinking about yourself.

I think one of the greatest rewards for the actor is to consequently develop a better understanding and acceptance of themselves. This is so because as *actors* experience a *character's* emotions, in rehearsal and in performance, they find that a lot of other stuff *comes up* about *them*. About how they feel. Their past. Their pain. Their guilt. For some, their nightmares or bad dreams or trauma. Some actors open *this*, let's call it, *this box*, and do this healing kind of work; others just ignore it.

Are you ready to get in touch with you? Because I suggest you jump right into *this box*. More on this later.

Taking the space

Taking the space means looking confident and owning where you are. Not looking out of place. It is a very important part of being an actor, because you are claiming your own energy, your own presence. It is also a very important part of auditioning and performing. Taking the space means you do not give your energy, presence or *power* away to someone else.

Why should we watch you as an actor? An audience will generally want to watch the actor if you take the space. If you walk in and look confident. If you perform with confidence. If you stand or sit with an open posture, with open body language, with your arms by your side, without crossing arms or legs, with your sternum up, with your head looking up and straight ahead.

Of course, this preferred way of using your body language is open for modification, as it might be necessary for you to close off your body language for a particular character.

But generally speaking, this behaviour will help you have presence and help you look confident, and consequently, help you with taking the space.

Talent and natural talent

I believe talent is doing well in your chosen field. Where an actor has intellect, a diligent eye to observe how people behave in life, some skills and creative ways of exploring as they perform. Most importantly, they are not afraid to perform.

Some people are born with natural talent. These people have an advantage. When you have natural talent, people want to watch you. Teachers and other industry people can see that you can do whatever they ask you to do; and you can do it very well.

Most actors develop their talents. With some actors, the talent that exists can blossom and grow when supported by a very good teacher.

I have trained and turned probably over a thousand actors into booking actors. One actor I taught went from being a beginner hiding in the back corners of a class of mine in Hollywood, into an award-winning actor who booked a lead in a feature film in Los Angeles.

Je ne sais quoi

Some people are just so interesting and watchable and often good-looking too, and so, they will work. Acting coaches can generally see people with an energy that attracts other people. These people usually have very good looks, a very good-looking body, and also confidence. This is so because they are used to being looked at and spoken to and often treated favourably. These people are often given other people's energy. What I mean by this is, as other people look at them, talk to them, look up to them, admire them, want to be with them, hang out with them – those onlookers give them their energy.

This type of person has an *unspoken something* about them. Meaning, we don't know what it is, but it is profoundly watchable. The French like to call it *je ne sais quoi*. These people will, most likely, simply work. Think Brad Pitt. Cary Grant. Hugh Grant. Halle Berry. Cate Blanchett. Tom Cruise. Shirley Temple.

So, if an acting teacher gets a young person with two or three of the above qualities mentioned in their class, they are generally going to work no matter who trains them. No disrespect to those actors I named above, or to their teachers.

Having taught actors since 1990, I can comfortably say, the better looking the actor is, the more they are likely to work in television. If they have *je ne sais quoi* too, the more they will work in all mediums.

Actors cannot all have the looks of a Halle Berry, Cary Grant or Brad Pitt, so please choose your teacher and their acting techniques well, and based on what they can teach you. For example, what they can teach you about personifying human behaviour, human heartache, risk-taking and creating characters.

After all, an actor should always remember this: acting is about the story and your character and their journey in the story and the relationships your character has with other characters. Acting is not about you.

> ### *Learning Point Number Two*
> - Work hard and smart on developing your talent and knowing how to hold and present yourself confidently with your mind, body and soul.
> - A little bit of fake it until you make it can be handy while you develop yourself and your skills and your inner self-confidence.

Chapter 3
Teaching: Theory and practice

In this chapter, I would like to talk a little about teaching and why your teacher is so important to you in your training.

What does the verb *to teach* mean? *The American Heritage® Dictionary of the English Language* gives six definitions:

1. *To impart knowledge or skill to: teaches children.*

2. *To provide knowledge of; instruct in: teaches French.*

3. *To condition to a certain action or frame of mind: teaching youngsters to be self-reliant.*

4. *To cause to learn by example or experience: an accident that taught me a valuable lesson.*

5. *To advocate or preach: teaches racial and religious tolerance.*

6. *To carry on instruction on a regular basis in: taught high school for many years. v.intr.to give instruction, especially as an occupation.*

(*The American Heritage® Dictionary of the English Language, Fourth Edition* copyright ©2000 by Houghton Mifflin Company. Updated in 2003. Published by Houghton Mifflin Company. All rights reserved.)

I would like to add a definition of my own: *to give* and *nurture*. A teacher is someone who gives and who nurtures the development of others.

Good and bad teachers

A poor teacher is one who just utters or spruiks (pitches to convince, for Americans) generalisations and industry-related clichés – such as "I love actors who take a risk", or "You didn't hit your arc in the scene" – without explaining what these comments mean; or who doesn't look at all the connotations of these comments.

As real specificity through utterances such as those above is a necessary component of communication between teacher and student.

When teaching, if a teacher does not explain themselves well, there's a breakdown in communication. I believe that one of the reasons why this type of *poor* teacher uses language that is not explained well is because they have no class objectives in their lesson plan when they teach. Often, they have no lesson plan either. Some people teaching students do not even know what a lesson plan is. Also, many teachers of actors are not even trained teachers.

With *no* lesson plan, no real learning points to teach the student in that lesson, the teacher is often out to just *talk at* the student, and does not really care about their growth. Sadly, this kind of teacher makes money based on their status or position in the entertainment industry.

An aside: I train all my teachers. Anyone who works for me learns my teaching way. They learn my curriculum. They learn that they must fully explain what cliché comments such as: "I love actors who take a risk" and "You didn't hit your arc in the scene" really mean.

Teachers should teach curriculum

I have a curriculum for teaching actors. It is very lengthy. I have lesson plans that come from my curriculum. I have objectives embedded in the lesson plans that actors should try to achieve in my classes.

I was taught the importance of curriculum, lesson planning and class objectives as a part of my University studies for my Bachelor of Education.

My curriculum is therefore based on my personal experiences, my education, my research, my intellect and my creativity.

A student can learn in a class of mine in the following ways:

- From objectives that I introduce in class
- From exercises that I introduce in class
- From what they experience when doing what I introduced in a class

- By watching others do the same thing in class
- By reflecting on the handouts that I give them in class (I'm a big handout teacher)
- By going home and discussing what they learnt with their family, friends or peers
- By seeing what I taught them in someone else outside of class. As actors personify human behaviour
- By seeing an actor on stage or on screen do what I taught them when they watch theatre or a film or TV show or a commercial
- By explaining what they learnt to others
- By teaching others what they have been taught

When I worked as an actor, I was lucky enough to be guided and nurtured. Is this what I have seen in my over forty years in the entertainment industry? Unfortunately, not always. To be frank, often not.

The wrong way to be taught

Just because someone has had success as, let's say, a recurring or series regular role on television for years, doesn't mean they can teach acting and/or teach you how to be an actor. The entertainment industry is full of so-called "experts" who try to teach actors; but they have no teaching training at all.

Most people, certainly parents, value the Bachelor of Education trained teacher at primary and secondary schools and the Masters and PhD trained teachers/lecturers at University. But for some reason, actors flock to so-called "industry professionals" or "experts" to teach them how to act.

That "industry professional" person may simply have found work as an actor because they were good-looking, charismatic and/or had a good body or bust size. Do you let an untrained dentist give you a filling? Do you let an untrained mechanic service your car?

I have experienced, witnessed and heard of profound verbal abuse by acting teachers or coaches (especially in LA and New York in the USA).

In those cases, untrained teachers ripped into actors and constantly put them down and then tried to re-direct or rebuild them.

For example, some teachers or coaches want to get to know their actors' negative or dramatic pasts. They do this and then bring it up and throw it at them verbally as provocation for a scene or for their acting development.

Other teachers are just downright abusive towards their students. Also, some teachers don't stop talking about themselves. About how good they are and/or they pretend to be teachers because of their own failures. I know of one unqualified teacher who covers their studio walls with pictures of themselves, not those of their students and their successes.

To be really specific: unfortunately, I have heard hundreds of times, that in particular, a very well-known American acting coach in Los Angeles puts down an actor, or gets his peers to put him down, to help him cry or be emotionally accessible.

The right way to be taught

Actors should be taught that being able to get in touch with their emotions and have emotional connection with their text begins with *breath* and not with abuse.

Not an onion or a lemon squeezed by the eye. Not by looking up to the theatre lights anymore. An actor's ability to breathe down into the body, especially into the body's chakra root area (the groin), is the way to go.

Wait, hang on, you might ask. But what about the actor who has just gone to those dark places that the poor teacher has insisted on getting them to go to? That is, the poor teacher who asked them about their past and then threw it back in their face or verbally abused them? Well, that actor's confidence could become unstable. Could receive *cell memory* damage of the mind, body and spirit (more on this later). Some would say, in a worst-case scenario, they could also become dependent on the abuser (in this case, their teacher). Maybe that is why the teacher is abusing them, because it helps pay their rent? Heavy, provocative comments I know.

If *you* experience an acting teacher/coach, or person who calls themselves a teacher or coach, who chooses to constantly put you down, no matter where you are living in the world, feel free to run for your life. Because, most likely, your self-esteem, confidence, thoughts, body and work will all be negatively affected.

A final note on this, to all those actors who have had a condescending, abusive, rude, obnoxious, selfish, know-it-all person teach them: read on, this book will change your world.

For all those actors who have had good guidance and nurturing please read on too!

A teacher who loves his job

I love my job. I love teaching. I have no hang-ups or regrets about my own past as an actor, except that I wish I had read a book like this when I was nineteen or so years old.

I have experienced some pretty tough stuff on my own journey in life so far. But this has all helped me to seek out education to be a better teacher, a better observer and learner, a better giver and a better person.

Whether you are a trained or untrained actor, an abused or nurtured actor, *you will find*, I humbly state, *you will be taught* to be a better actor the Australian way by reading this book and doing the exercises you'll find along the way.

I believe and work in the following theoretical areas with actors: metaphysics, philosophy, spirit, theory, practice, energy and positivity.

Teaching in three main human condition areas

My experiences as an actor, teacher and director have led me into forming three main areas of teaching study.

Psychology
- What's going on in your mind

Physiology
- How the body works
- How to use your body with breath
- Breath, thought, image, voice connection

Physiognomy
- How to use the head, the face and the eyes, especially for the camera

Curriculum teaches in three main areas

- **Structure (subject)**
    - Acting Techniques x five
    - How to connect with text x eight
    - Creating Characters x four
    - Role Playing x two
    - Improvisation x four
    - Breath and Voice x eight
    - Movement x 2

- On Camera x eight
- Performing for the frame topics for self-tapes x 2
- Neutral Mask
- Performance
- Risk-taking x 2
- Your Style Appeal
- Business Side of Acting x two

- **Making choices**
  - Scene study/scene analysis x four
  - Background to scene and character x two
  - Surroundings – the start/moment before
  - Character choices – including wants, opinions, attitude, points of concentration

- **Let go, relax, trust, play, enjoy**
  - Audition Preparation and Training x four
  - The right mindset to relax, trust, play and enjoy yourself in performance
  - Audition performance x four
  - Taking the re-direction in an audition

I find that with my philosophy and curriculum, I give the actor the best training that I can. I am working with them from the beginning, all the way to the audition.

Of course, for my private students, this includes prepping them for the work after they have booked the job and then reviewing the work, once it airs on stage or screen.

My mindset

Whether I am with family or friends or by myself; I love myself. I reward myself by resting, by watching my favourite television shows or films, or by going to the theatre, watching Australian football or cricket. I give to me by talking to my family and friends, sitting on the beach, kissing my beautiful wife, reading great literature or by writing this book. Whatever it takes to help me give to me.

By doing so, I feel I am free and open and willing to give to others. I often feel I am channelled by the universe as I educate and give to others. I know this may sound a little corny or silly, but I feel it.

I love teaching and coaching others to be better actors and better people. I get excited when they call me saying that they got a call back, or they booked the job, or they implemented stuff they learnt in class, or in a private session; and they feel that they have grown. This is as good as giving me, their teacher, an apple.

"Giving the teacher an apple" – I really like this saying as it is a *symbol for imparting knowledge* and makes me feel good and acknowledges in some small way, the journey that we, the student and I, are both on together.

How I develop an actor's self-love

I believe that everybody has the ability to act, and *my* philosophy on teaching/coaching actors is very much grounded in the subtle developing of a student's inner *you*. Empowering actors to know themselves. Along the way I also teach them acting techniques and skills. As well as a preferred way to think and behave.

An actor in tune with themselves is less likely to be out to gain acceptance or love from others. As he should develop self-love and not seek it from anyone.

An actor in tune with themselves will create stronger, more in-depth characters.

An actor in tune with themselves, who loves himself, and knows about himself, will get the most out of learning and implementing the Australian techniques that I teach and the chakra alignment and emotional exercise work that I teach.

An actor in tune with themselves, who loves himself, and knows about himself, will have their mind in a much clearer space to make choices:

in preparation, during the audition, during the re-direction from the casting director and on set.

An actor in tune with themselves is in a much stronger position to accept the rejections that are inevitable in this profession.

An actor who loves himself is less likely to put people who have power over him on a pedestal.

Think of the people who have power over the actor: the casting directors, famous directors or big-name actors already cast in a project. Also think of: successful or popular television shows or films, or an actor's targeted television shows or films. If an actor puts the casting director, or the project that they are going for, or any person, on a pedestal, they are "sacredising". Sacredising is common with actors and they shouldn't do it because it affects their nerves and their concentration.

As a teacher, what do I do?

In both my private one-on-one teachings and group classes, I use lesson plans that I have devised to train actors. Just by doing the exercises from the lesson plans in class, the students are improving their acting. Please see pages 251 to 253 for a sample lesson plan that I use in my acting school. The plans, which are based on a curriculum, have specific objectives that the students have to try to obtain in class.

I say to the students in the school: "If I don't say anything to you specifically in class, it means I like what you are doing". This is very important because with my teaching guidance, I will build the students' confidence and trust from within them.

I work on empowering the student. I do this because I want the student to build their craft from within and because, as a teacher, I cannot come into the audition room and stand by the actor's side and tell them what to do or say. Or how to do and say it. So, the stronger the actor is from within, the better they will do.

Occasionally, I will contact an actor out of class and give them specific tasks that I would like them to work on to improve their work. But until this happens, I say to the actor, "Remember just by doing the work in each lesson, you will be improving your acting because there are objectives embedded in the lesson plans".

I let actors explore. I let them play. I let them choose and make their own decisions about their interpretations of the text. Then I guide them where necessary with all my knowledge.

I do this also because all scripts and all characters have a journey. Actors need to trust that they can act as their characters on that journey. Too many actors try to control every moment of that journey and in doing so, are not that watchable.

As I am building the inner confidence from within the actor, sometimes it is best to say nothing and to encourage them to keep exploring. Encourage them to keep discovering, keep putting themselves out there with their work and their interpretations, without constantly monitoring or telling them how to do something better.

The teacher is not working on *their acting* or on *them* being cast in the part. Consequently, a couple of questions I would like to ask some other acting teachers is, "As a teacher, why teach the actor to act the way you would do it? Why insist they perform your interpretation of the scene?"

Actors, I suggest that you search on YouTube for some successful teachers' promo videos, especially American teachers/coaches. You will see videos of many teachers telling the actors how to interpret the scene. Their emphasis is not on developing the actors' acting skills, but much more so on telling the actor how they should interpret the scene.

If this is the focus of their teachings, and I have been told by many actors that it is, this is not actor training; it is an English literature comprehension class.

This always amazes me, as many students deem this type of behaviour to be good actor training. Some actors stick with this type of teacher in class because the student is most likely determining that this is a good example of the teacher's intellect. In other words, they think, "I should do it this way, and aren't they smart for telling me so?" So, the student follows or copies the teacher. This seems folly to me.

If you follow this philosophy and do what the teacher says here, you are mirroring his performance or personifying only his perspective. What is going to happen when you get an audition, and he is unavailable to work with you on the comprehension of the scene?

As well as with your teacher, share your audition script with family and friends and get their opinions. Yes, do listen to their opinions, but do try to create your own views, your own work, your own way, your own character; it will be more believable, as *your* interpretation is very important.

An aside: Make a rule that you will always Google the play, Google the literature, Google the writer, Google the TV show or the film; and educate yourself on a play's themes or a writer's main contentions. Empower yourself.

In support of this, I believe that the best literature in the world is ambiguous – open to many different interpretations. So, why would a teacher impose *their* interpretation of the scene as the only way in which to do a scene? Especially for an audition.

I propose these teachers/coaches don't have acting training lesson plans that contain objectives for students to achieve. I also propose that they want the actor dependent on them. So they keep making money from that student.

A purpose or walking blindly?

Having some acting talent is not enough. Your chance for a successful career depends on what is going on in your mind. Are you prepared to let a teacher get to know some of what's going on up there?

Let me ask you this: do you constantly go from one acting school in your town to another? I call this "cruising the schools".

How can anyone develop a particular teacher's technique that works for them if they cruise the schools? Can you, as an actor, build on developing that technique if you cruise the schools? Can you develop a rapport with a teacher you know and like if you cruise the schools?

The answers to those questions should be clear. Simply put, you can do yourself more harm than good by cruising the schools.

If you are in an acting class and studying for three hours a night, one night a week, for four weeks – well, that is not that much studying, is it?

Can you be very well trained in that time? Sure, you'll learn things, but really your relationship is just getting established with the teacher in these first twelve hours.

From personal experience, it can often take a while for the teacher to find out a student's level of talent, habits, commitment, passion, flexibility, intellect, knowledge, professionalism and psychological state.

A good teacher thinks: what is the best way to work with each individual? What ways work best for them? For you?

The beauty of full-time teaching from a qualified teacher – whether it be in a primary or secondary school, or in a full-time college for a year – is that the teacher gets a substantial amount of time in which to build trust and rapport. A teacher requires a substantial amount of time to tap into the psychology of each individual and pass over knowledge. Using that time, the teacher can maximise the teaching of the student to help them improve.

I always seek to develop this type of relationship with the actors I teach. The reason I have brought up this topic is because, generally speaking, lots of actors constantly cruise different acting schools.

I must admit, I get frustrated if this happens with students in my classes. I always like to give actors the best platform for them to achieve their goals. To do that, I need time with them.

In closing on talking about my teaching philosophy, science and psychology tell us that no two human beings are the same. Not even twins. Consequently, no two actors are the same. What works for one, may not work for another. Actors will learn and grow in different ways.

One of the lovely challenges when teaching actors is to find the best way to train each one of them. What I like about teaching actors is the *potpourri* of choices that I can give them, including different techniques.

I always say to actors, "You will decide what works best for you. What helps you book work".

As I teach actors I think, "If I have helped the actors develop their acting skills, their decisions of character and scene, their techniques, their awareness of industry factors to help them book professional paid work, then I am doing my job. I have empowered them."

I am the type of teacher who will get you to *participate* when you are in class. Yes, there is always theory. But you will need to participate. As the teacher I am a conduit. A conduit between the student and the paid work they seek. I believe you learn the most by doing.

There are many hundreds of experienced, respected and successful acting teachers worldwide today, teaching many different acting techniques. I teach and train actors by drawing on my acting experiences and my years as a teacher. I teach with my intellect, heart, listening skills, care, creativity, curriculum, sense of humour, firmness at times, soul, humbleness, honesty and an open mind. I give the students the best I can. I give actors variety and choices.

> ### *Learning Point Number Three*
> - Choose a non-abusive, and ideally, a professionally trained teacher.
> - Always ask yourself: What have I learnt today from this teacher?
> - Be open to seriously getting to know yourself; you'll be a stronger and better actor for it.

Developing the inner you

The rewards for developing *real* inner self-confidence and faith and trust, cannot be under-estimated. Inner self-confidence will permeate your demeanour, personality and acting work. It will ultimately replace the *act* of being confident or the "fake it till you make it" persona that you may have had going beforehand.

Later chapters of this book contain exercises on developing the inner you, and developing confidence from within you.

Cell memory

I once went to an audition and thought: "I feel like I have been here before". Not at this specific audition, but I've *felt* like this before.

If my audition experience was poor – feeling very nervous or anxious, or distracted in the mind, or feeling insecure about my choices with the work – I would often feel that my body had remembered a past negative experience of feeling nervous or anxious, distracted, or of not trusting my choices.

Sometimes this sense of having been here before stemmed from an experience at an acting class with a teacher. Sometimes it was from an audition. In a worst-case scenario, the pressure and anxiety that I was feeling at the audition made me think that I was not worthy of any success. I felt that I didn't deserve it because I didn't love myself enough.

Many actors have told me that they feel they have had these negative thoughts and experiences too.

At this point I would like to introduce the concept of *cell memory*. Our bodies are composed of millions of cells, and some psychologists and scientists theorise that cells have memory. That is, memories exist not just in brain cells but in body cells too. I should point out that this is not scientifically proven.

Many psychologists and scientists link cells to both our physiological and psychological states. They stipulate that positive affirmations, constructive criticism, and other verbal and non-verbal support will all affect a person's confidence.

Simply considering that body cells may have some links to our memory is fascinating stuff. The point I am making here is that if cells in our bodies have some links to *memory*, then mental abuse from a teacher/coach (just like mental abuse from a parent) could damage us and affect our confidence, our thinking and, consequently, our performances.

If we have had bad experiences, the cells in our bodies might remember those. Later on in life, if we encounter a similar situation, our cells could remember that *past bad experience* and cause problems for us.

I am bringing this up because this could, in turn, affect your acting career.

I ask you to recall a time when you didn't enjoy being in an acting class. Why was it a bad experience? Were you anxious because you were being verbally abused? Well, if the answer is *yes*, when you act next, it is possible that it is not going to be a positive experience for you. Unless, that is, the mind and body and cells are reprogrammed from within you.

In support of this, if you are vulnerable to begin with, god help you after an acting teacher has repeatedly verbally abused you, or put you down, or asked you about your bad emotional past and then verbally thrown it back in your face in an acting class.

If you have had past negative feelings, perhaps a heightened sense of anxiety in an audition, or you felt like you were being judged by your fellow actors, then it is most likely because your cells were remembering a past similar experience. Fear and anxiety have come back to influence you again.

I believe our cells have memory. To prevent a negative experience happening again, you need to work on the inner you. Give yourself a positive experience of working on that scene, or whatever the situation is, and/or give yourself some other kind of positive psychological experience.

For example, you could perform for peers or family or a teacher that you know will support you and only give you positive reinforcement and constructive criticism.

I call this "healing work", and I do it both directly and indirectly in my classes. Healing work is important because many actors unfortunately choose teachers who are abrupt and so tough on them that it causes them to cry, lose concentration, stop trusting their instincts, and generally negatively affect their listening and acting.

Unfortunately, some teachers are so abusive and destructive that some actors give up acting altogether.

Some actors think this is the right way to be taught. That they have to be treated harshly, and so only respect teachers or coaches who criticise them. I know this because dozens upon dozens of times I've had to fix up self-esteem and confidence problems of actors caused by these experiences.

I don't really know why an actor would want to be in a class where a teacher yells and screams at them and even calls them names. Perhaps they don't know better. Perhaps they are just like sheep, following other actors.

Here's a metaphor that seems apt: many people eat takeaway food and have sugary soft drinks that are proven to cause damage to the human body. I'm sure some psychologists would say that these people do this simply because other people do it.

This is not how I or my staff teach. I care about my actors' growth and successes, no matter how large or small. I guide the actor. I teach them practical things to work on to help them improve their skills because I do not want damage done. I do not want to damage their cells, because body cells have memory. If, hypothetically, I did treat them poorly, I believe that the bad experience will most likely resurface, maybe in that audition for the job they really want. I believe that care, *really teaching* and loving is the way to go. Not creating fear and dependence.

People are attracted to positive people. People are attracted to people who succeed. People are attracted to people with confidence. Especially inner confidence, which permeates the body and radiates outwards into the world to help create your aura. When I teach, I work on building a person's inner confidence, so that the actor can have that all-round confidence. This is one of the main reasons why I talk about developing the inner you in this book.

With this inner confidence, you will then be more likely to not only succeed as an actor, but also be more likely to take risks and push and challenge yourself in your actor training development, in classes, in workshops, on the set, and, in fact, in all aspects of your life.

This is the case because you have worked on the negative past experiences inside your mind and body. You have worked on healing yourself. Because you believe you can. Because you are working on being infallible. Because you can take the knockbacks and rejections, of not getting the work in an audition, for example. Because you feel you can take on anything and you can look forward to these challenges, rather than fear them.

You must work on that inner confidence. I suggest you work with a teacher who will be honest with you, as well as subtly push your boundaries and guide you.

No one should strip you down because they think that is the way to teach someone. Or because of their own insecurities. Or for their own ego. Or because they are using shock tactics and histrionics because they have built a career doing so.

> ### Learning Point Number Four
> - Choose your teacher wisely.
> - Make sure they encourage and empower you with practical skills that you can implement.
> - Work on the inner you, get in tune with yourself, so you have strength and resilience upon which to build your career.

Developing the right thought patterns

From my experiences as an actor, from hearing stories from peers, from watching peers and from teaching and coaching actors since 1990, I consistently come across actors who self-sabotage and procrastinate.

In doing so, they are standing in the way of their own acting progression and success.

Here are some examples of self-sabotage and procrastination that I have had to assist the actor with. You:

- tell people that you are an actor but you are not in class working on your skills
- don't get together with other actors and work on scenes and characters
- don't take advantage of the huge number of ways you can get yourself auditions. For example, accessing auditions has increased tenfold with the internet
- don't go out and try to get an agent or a manager
- don't get headshots taken with your new hair cut or colour
- don't type up a résumé
- don't join the unions (important in the USA)

- don't network in the entertainment industry

Actors sabotage in their own minds too. Here are some examples of what they say:

- I'm not good enough
- I'm not pretty enough
- I'm not slim enough
- My breasts are not big enough
- I'm not tall enough
- I have an accent
- I have a lazy eye
- I don't have family in the industry
- I'm not Jewish
- Do I have to sleep with an agent, manager, casting director or director to get work?
- I won't get another job to help pay for my class or my headshots
- I need help
- I need a sugar daddy or mummy
- I'm not a good enough actor
- I'm not creative
- I'm too argumentative
- I don't like working with people
- I like to speak my mind too much
- I need my *ducks in a row* before I move forward
- Poor me

In class I have come across actors who sabotage their own development. For example, some have said the following to me, or told others who have told me that they have said these things:

- The teacher doesn't like me
- The teacher doesn't think I'm any good
- The teacher hasn't said anything to me tonight or for a while, which means I must be doing a bad job or I mustn't be any good

- My peers in class don't like me
- My peers in class are all trying to get me into bed
- I won't do the homework (so when I perform the scene and don't do a good job, I can say it's because I didn't do the homework)
- I'll consistently turn up late to class (so I have an excuse as to why I'm not so good, or to take the pressure off myself when I perform)
- I'll be inconsistent with my attendance (so if I don't do a good job, I can blame it on that)
- I can create dramas in my life, perhaps not totally true stories (so I can use that as an excuse as to why I wasn't fantastic)

The list could go on and on as to how some actors procrastinate and self-sabotage in an industry that will not stand by and wait for them. Some actors consistently put themselves at a disadvantage before they even begin. Before they are even considered for roles.

Why do actors do this? It is slightly different for each actor, but I've found that there are often similarities. Similarities usually linked to self-esteem, sabotage and procrastination. In particular, their self-esteem with links to their beliefs, has usually got something to do with it.

The things they need to learn, their behaviour, their thoughts are all linked in with their *psyche*. The thoughts in their mind, body and soul. If you are making the choice to act, I can only encourage you to make the choice to consider working on yourself. If you can relate to any of the above listed examples of procrastination and self-sabotage, I strongly suggest you *take a look* at the inner *you*.

Work on you, your psyche, and you will self-sabotage and procrastinate less, and achieve your goals much quicker in your life. This is my first main gift to you on this journey through this book; work on the inner you.

How do you take a look at the inner you? Here are some suggestions:

- Meditate

- Work on breathing deeply into the body and doing emotional exercises(see pages 91 to 94) and/or chakra work (see pages 88 to 91)
- Do yoga
- Do the chair exercise – where you put two chairs opposite one another and ask yourself questions in one chair and then get up and move to the other chair and answer the questions. Continue moving between the two chairs until you have nothing to say. Then reflect
- Do self-hypnosis (see pages 139 to 141)
- Write. Ask yourself questions and just write the responses without editing in your mind. Let the stream of consciousness come out of you onto the paper. For example: why am I not getting new headshots done? Why am I not really preparing for an audition? Why am I just trying to wing it?
- Try writing a question with your dominate hand and then answer the question with your non-dominant hand. By doing so, you will be accessing another part of your brain. Keep asking yourself to be specific and ignore the tardy writing of your non-dominant hand. The answers you receive will be golden
- Read self-development books, for example by Louise Hay. Or read specific self-help books, like Albert Ellis's *How To Control Your Anxiety Before It Controls You* or *Seat of The Soul* by Gary Zukav
- You could see a psychologist or psychiatrist
- You could consider attending a class that teaches the importance of breath work and gets you to work on the inner you, while doing your actor training

Learning Point Number Five

- What does your mind say to you?
- Get in touch with who you are.
- If you procrastinate and self-sabotage, try to fix this.
- Work with your emotions and try to have positive thoughts – thoughts that come from love and not fear.

Chapter 4
Training the actor: Introducing Australian techniques

One of the techniques that I adapted came from people who trained me. I call this technique "Australian techniques – Dropping In The Text". Therefore, what I call *Australian techniques* is a curriculum of classes developed by me, based on my experiences as an actor, acting student, director and teacher, dating back to 1977. The other four techniques that I teach are listed and talked about in Chapter 5, International Theorists.

I wrote my school AIDA's curriculum. Some of the Australian techniques classes were influenced by some excellent teachers. In particular, David Latham and Bill Pepper, as well as the respected Scottish teacher Kristin Linklater.

In Australia, I have studied and/or worked with: Roger Hodgman, Lindy Davies, Bill Pepper, David Latham and Paul Hampton, and briefly with Dean Carey and Aarne Neeme.

All of these teachers have worked for respected schools in Australia. Past graduates from these schools include: Cate Blanchett, Judy Davis, Mel Gibson, Hugh Jackman, Miranda Otto, Hugo Weaving, Sam Worthington and Jason Clarke. Russell Crowe worked with a voice teacher from one of these schools.

Above: The AIDA school on Santa Monica Boulevard in Hollywood, Los Angeles in 2010.

Why "Australian techniques"?

The world is fully exploring the power of, and the impact made by, the Australian actor and Australian actor training.

An example of the popularity of Australian actors can be seen in the fact that there is an Australian actor, as a series regular, in so many television shows in the USA. There are also hundreds more in films in the USA too. This has been going on for many years now.

Above: The AIDA company profile from 2006.

Classical training and my school

From my experiences in teaching, and to a lesser extent in acting (where I have experienced going to schools or classes), and from what many hundreds of students have told me, dating back to the 1990s, many schools or classes that teach acting have no focus. No curriculum. No, or very little, structure or principles at all. Many schools and classes are simply out to take an actor's money.

I can categorically state, as I have been told by *hundreds* of students in the USA and Australia and a few students in Japan, that some acting schools and acting classes use a "band aid" approach to acting: they give the students predominantly external training. For example, the vocal work that they do is focused on diction more so than anything else.

I believe that if actors continually have external training only, they will pay their money to a school that offers part- or full-time training, for a year or so, or do ongoing classes, and most of them will come out and not receive industry representation from a manager or agent and also have no career. I see and hear of this time and time again. I have personally witnessed this, or been told about it, by multiple hundreds of students for over two decades.

It is not easy for me to write about this topic as I know it is provocative, negative and making judgement calls on some acting schools and classes in the entertainment industry. But it needs to be said. Actors need to know that they are often, simply, being ripped off by some acting schools and classes.

So, choose your acting school and teacher/coach wisely.

On a brighter note, you might be surprised to read that many of the best actors in the world have had classical training. What I mean by "classical training" is that actors have had extensive training on breath and voice. How to breathe into the body, where to breathe into the body, how to project and articulate and give flavour with the voice and how to link breath with voice and how to use their breath and voice to make impact as an actor. They have also learnt about script analysis, improvisation, imagination, movement, external stimulus and the works of Stanislavski.

This is one of the reasons why respected Australian acting schools do so well. For the best schools, their training work begins with where the actor breathes in the body.

I'm very strong on classical training and on the grounding of the actor. I mentioned in Chapter 3 the three areas of study that I teach, but I would like to repeat them here because they are so prominent in my teachings:

- Psychology
- Physiology
- Physiognomy

A far as psychology is concerned, I find I am always talking to the student about what goes on in their minds. So much so, that I say to students, what goes on in your mind, the thoughts that you have, will profoundly influence whether you work or not, whether or not you book a lot of work.

Physiology means how the body works. How we use breath and voice to connect with ourselves and with our text.

Physiognomy is about how we use our head, our face, our eyes and lips on screen, especially in the mid-shot, the close-up and extreme close-up.

Above: This AIDA group includes seven times award-winning actor Naama Kates, along with Adam Jennings, Erica Pitts, Sam Aaron and Lauren Simon.

Above: This Wednesday-night group, called the "Cold Chisel" group, includes successful award-winning actors: Cyanne McClairian (seven times-award-winner on stage) and Michelle Massey-Bedell (Best Actress in a Feature Film at the Pasadena Film Festival in 2007). As well as actor and award-winning film producer Chris Ivan Cevic, international producer Jennifer Hutchins and actors Tanayi Seabrook and Rebecca Brooks.

How are Australian techniques different?

To begin with, the mere fact that I grew up in Australia and had experiences as an actor, acting student, director and teacher living within Australia up until 2000 means to me that the curriculum that I had devised and the classes that I have taught, would be Australian techniques.

The eight points listed below are subject topics of the Australian techniques that I teach:

- How to stand and sit
- Breathing through the mouth as well as the nose
- Breath work – deep into the body
- Breath work linking in with the physiological connection with emotion
- Breath – thought – image – voice connection
- Chakra exercises
- Emotional exercises
- Dropping In The Text – layering the text into the body

How are Australian techniques different? I think the best way to answer this question is to say that the work that I do is both internal and external. In support of this, the work links breath, thought, image and voice. We naturally do these things in life. We breathe, get thoughts, often summon images and then we speak.

Breath and voice

When I was in acting and teaching training at University from 1987 to 1991, our voice teacher, a woman, used to jokingly say, "I want you all to breathe into and from your vaginas". She then set about teaching us, females and males, how to breathe down into the body, including into our genital areas.

From my experiences in Australia, at the most respected schools, there is a huge emphasis on breath and voice training. Questions I have been asked by students over the years include: "Why is breath work so important? How can your ability to breathe deeply into your body and access as much of your body with breath affect your voice and ultimately your performance?"

In general, one important difference between the trained and the untrained actor is that the untrained actor often has their breath centred across their shoulders and in their neck, chest and jaw.

They breathe and speak from within their shoulders and the neck. This is often personified by tense shoulders, vein lines on the side of their neck and red faces when they raise their voices, or run out of breath, or get angry.

This is best exemplified in theatre if they try to project with their voice. And this is worsened if they spend too much time in the gym. Especially if they constantly work on their back and shoulder muscles. This type of actor often speaks with a higher than normal or preferred *pitched* speaking *v*oice.

They often also find it more difficult to display emotion and, most importantly, find it difficult to connect their breath and their voice with their text. This is so because they are tensing all their muscles by activating and swelling/strengthening them, and most likely, they are not aware that they need to breathe down into their bodies.

In support of this, they may not realise that it is harder to get *voice resonation* from muscles that are tense, tight and activated into a state of tension.

Above: Actors working on their breath and voice with Paul in an AIDA class in Hollywood, USA.

My breath and voice education, readings, practice and teachings are extensive. From Kristin Linklater and Bill Pepper to David Latham and Cecily Berry. As well as elocution teachers, meditation teachers and the Indian Sanskrit chakra work. As well as doctors and psychologists.

An actor should do this breath work to make connections with themselves. Their breath with their body. Actors do this work to achieve non-resistance. They work with releasing all the habitual tensions that they hold and release those tensions to help facilitate emotional connection and imaginary freedom.

Some questions an actor should ask themselves concerning their voice and breath include:

- What happens in my mind prior to speaking?
- How important is my voice?
- How important is it to work the facial muscles, the tongue muscles, the shoulder, neck and jaw muscles?
- How important is it to work the articulators in the mouth?
- How does working all these muscles influence the voice?
- How does working all these muscles influence the pitch, projection, tone, placement and flavour of the voice?
- When is it best to turn the voice on? Meaning, use its capabilities, its range?
- How to adapt the voice for roles as a working-class, middle-class or upper-class person?
- Do you change your voice for theatre, film and TV use? If so, how?
- How important is it to convey what you're doing with your emotions?
- How to find your voice. How can we find *your* voice? Noting and addressing the following:
    - range
    - emotional content
    - energy

- volume
- pitch
- how to use the voice for effect
- pacing
- high – medium – low levels of the use of voice
- articulation and diction
- If I improvise, I often do very good work first time with my voice. Why is that?
- How can I layer the work into my body, where I can connect with the words, feelings and attitudes from a script?
- What do we naturally do as a human being regarding breath, thought, image, voice, connection?

Actors should work on the voice, getting it at a level where they can switch it on and off and know at what level they are speaking: low, medium or high. For example, an actor would speak at a low volume level for a dramatic feature film close-up. Whereas performing a Shakespeare play on stage and projecting to the back of the theatre would require an actor to speak at a high level of volume.

- My breath and voice training works in the following areas:
- How to breathe and how to use your breath
- Breath, thought, image, voice, connection
- Breathing deeply into the body, including into the back, bum, genital areas and chakra points
- Voice articulation
- Voice diction
- Voice tone and pitch
- Voice projection
- Finding your voice and using voice to your advantage

Connecting breath, thought, image and voice

In life, our mind and bodies work naturally to form and produce a level of breath, thought, image and voice connection.

What this means is: we breathe normally, depending on the situation. We have thoughts in our mind and they are often linked to images and ultimately to our voice, and then we speak.

The actor must work on getting their breath down into their body to help them connect, including to emotionally connect, with their text and their feelings or *acted* feelings.

Connecting with our text means having the ability to seem like what we are saying is real. When doing this well, the audience really believes that what is going on really *is* going on and what is being said really *is* being said.

This is often a challenge for the actor. I cannot stress enough the importance of being able to access as much of your body as possible with breath as this will give you a platform on which to build your connection.

Also, accessing your body with breath is healthy living. It will help release stress and anxiety and possibly reduce the risk of subluxations in your back. Subluxations are problems that chiropractors, or muscle workers such as masseurs, work on, to try and get knots out of you and/or align your spine.

So the actor must work on breathing into their bodies all the time. An actor must work a few times a week on getting the breath down into their body, and then practise every now and then to keep their skills up. Below are a few examples to help you do this:

- Catch yourself in everyday life breathing into the upper part of the body (this could even include as if you feel like you have just completed a run)
- Drop breath in through the open mouth

- Encourage yourself to drop the breath down into the body. You do this by simply opening the mouth slightly and trying to breathe into your diaphragm and/or your lower back.
- Spend time on your back on the floor with your knees bent and think down into your body – like a bucket dropping down into a well to fetch a pail of water, or water falling down a waterfall
- Read books on how the breath affects a person's body
- Live your life thinking, mouth open and slight smile. The slight smile will make it easier to breathe down into the body as it helps open up the back of the throat
- Meditate
- Work on aligning your chakras (see page 90). Most importantly, work with the root chakra, which is the key to emotional connection. It is around the pubic bone/pubic hair/genital area
- Get an acting coach who sees the importance of breath work to help you get breath, thought, image, voice connection with your text

As acting begins with breath work, actors should work to release tension from their bodies and open themselves up to breathe the way they did when they were infants. Have you ever seen a newborn baby breathe? The whole body breathes, the whole body moves. Watch a baby's feet move as it breathes.

That was you once. What happened? Life. Life's problems, rejections, fears, insecurities, your posture and perhaps behavioural repetitions and physical ailments. All these things affected you and your ability to breathe deeply into the body.

If you link the breath work with chakra work and emotional exercises, you will soon start to get in touch with the inner you. With regular work you should begin to learn to experience emotional connection on cue. This means, by dropping the breath into your body, you will be able to trigger yourself to be emotional.

After a few months you should easily be performing scenes and monologues with emotional clarity and with more honesty. This is only the beginning. This is very empowering.

As actors feel they can cry on cue and feel connected with their breath, they generally feel they have much more of an emotional range to draw on and give as a performer.

Always remember, audiences nowadays want and need to see the characters they watch be vulnerable!

Imagery

The challenges for the actor are to work with the text in a way in which our mind and body naturally work. Hence the:

- emphasis on breath work
- breath, thought, image, voice, connection work
- Dropping In The Text work
- warm-up work
- root and other chakra connection work
- emotional exercises

When Dropping In The Text, I often talk to actors about *seeing* the images of the text. For example, "All the world's a stage". Are you seeing people from all around the world? Are you seeing a stage? What is a stage? What is the world?

By being pedantic, it helps the actor with thinking about the images and helps them with their breath, thought, image and voice connection.

Voice

I have written already about the importance of your voice when I talked about *the inner you* and *breath, thought, image, voice* connection.

I would like to elaborate a little more here so you are aware of some ways of behaviour that I suggest you don't do, and some ways of thinking and exercises that I suggest you do do.

The voice is a powerful instrument. Some actors restrict their chances of getting work due to the lack of quality of their voice in terms of articulation, diction, pitch, volume, and their general sound or tone.

Some actors restrict their chances of getting work because they simply cannot be heard; they need work with projection.

Some actors restrict their chances of getting work because their upbringing was in another country and no matter how hard they try, they just can't sound like, for example, an Aussie in the Australian bush.

I work with actors on their voices because the quality of their voices helps them book work. As said, my voice work is a culmination of linking the breath work, the breathing into the body work, the opening up of the channels through mouth open and slight smile, and the freeing and relaxing of the passages in which the voice can pass through.

Good posture is essential for the actor as it makes it easier to breathe down into the body. My work loosens the muscles in the upper body, the jaw, the shoulders, the neck and the upper back. I then get the actor down onto the floor and I get them to breathe into their diaphragms, their bums and ultimately into their pubic bone areas. I do this using a series of exercises with the student. (Please see page 90 for some of the exercises.)

The pubic bone–genital area is the actor's core centre for breath. The root chakra is also there too (see pages 90 to 91).

The smart actor, as well as disc jockeys and voice-over actors, uses their voice for effect.

Being an actor wanting to improve your voice, I suggest you start by thinking of the topics listed here:

- How can I improve my breath support?
- How can I achieve breath, thought, image, voice connection?
- How can I articulate with my voice?
- How can I improve my diction?

- How can I develop the subtleties of tone and inclination? (a very powerful tool for film and television acting)
- How can I improve my voice projection and my use of pitch?
- How can I develop the voice through singing?

With text, you should think, how can I work and improve my voice and breath support with the following:

- Scripts – film/TV scripts, plays, articles.
- Poetry such as Shakespeare's sonnets or from poetry books.
- Tongue-twisting exercises such as: "Betty bought a bit of butter, but the butter Betty bought was bitter, said Betty, if I buy a bit of better butter my batter will be better, so Betty bought a bit of better butter and her batter was better".
- Anything the actors can pick up and read.

For example: with projection exercises, you can go from lying on your back, developing the breath support by encouraging yourself to drop the breath in through the mouth and down into the diaphragm; and then use this breath to assist your voice as you breathe out. In time, you will eventually be able to stand on a busy street and project poetry or text out towards an imaginary audience, who are a fair distance away from you.

An aside: in the USA I used to do an exercise where the actors were on the other side of the road from me, outside of the theatre, across Santa Monica Boulevard in Hollywood. The actors had to stand on one side of the street, with their hands on their lower backs (the back side of their diaphragms), and project their voices out across the busy street towards me.

My mentor of many years, the late and great character actor Reg Evans, used to say, "Acting is all about voice, voice, voice!"

To help get yourself going and heading towards having a better voice:

- Record your voice to see how it sounds

- Take notes on someone's voice that you like. The same gender as you
- Listen to the BBC Radio live, online, from the UK. The presenters generally enunciate very well. They have lovely diction, rich deep vocal tones and a lower speaking pitch of voice
- Think, I'm going to get breath down into my body
- I'm going to work on articulation exercises
- I'll concentrate on pronouncing my consonants and vowels
- I'll read books on improving my voice
- I'll try to speak well
- I'll read more, as this will improve my vocabulary. I'll read Shakespeare, including his sonnets
- I'll join a public speaking group or form a similar group

A way of being: Developing the right habits

I suggest you try to live your life following the principles listed below, as you will be developing the right behavioural patterns by opening up your body and consequently making it easier for you to do the exercises. Remember, what we do in life, we will do as an actor.

I propose:

- Stand tall. Keep your body straight with your sternum up – it is much harder to get breath into the body when the sternum is collapsed
- Often wiggle your jaw, shoulders and hips, to keep them loose
- Try to always have open body language. That is, try to not continually cross your arms or legs. Not only does it make it harder to breathe down into the body, you also don't look so happy, and your metaphysical energy surrounding your body is closed off. Keep it open so the Universe can reward you for your hard work
- Try to live your life walking around with your mouth slightly open and with a slight smile. This will help you drop the breath naturally into the body

- Take these behaviours into your daily life, for example when a car that you are travelling in pulls up at the traffic lights, do a physical check and make sure that your jaw is loose, your mouth is open and that you are dropping breath down into your body through your mouth. This will help you develop these patterns of behaviour.
- In addition, adjust your steering wheel in your car and/or adjust your computer chair, so that you are not activating your trapezius shoulder muscles into a state of tension and causing unnecessary tension in your shoulders.

Paul Parker's warm-ups

The following exercises should be done every second day or so for about a month and then once a week for a year or so. They should take approximately one hour to do. By doing these exercises you will start to teach yourself how to release tension from the upper body and make it easier to breathe down into the body. Some of the origins of these exercises come from Kristin Linklater, Bill Pepper and David Latham.

Massaging the jaw

Massage the subtle indentation where the upper and lower jaw meet, about an inch up from the bottom of each ear. Then massage down the jaw to the chin, along the lower jaw and along the upper jaw to the nose. Give an extra good rub in spots that feel tender or have a lump as you may have a knot in a facial muscle.

Cupping the jaw

Place your hands on the lower jaw. Open and close the lower jaw, first with cupped hands, then with one finger on the chin. Then, open and close the upper jaw tilting your head backward while keeping the lower jaw immobile(even though this sounds silly, this part of the exercise is similar in fashion to the little man in the Reach toothbrush television commercial). First with cupped hands holding the lower jaw in place, then with one finger on the chin.

Loosening the jaw

Cup your hands together. Shake and loosen the jaw and face muscles by shaking the jaw as you shake the hands. Make some freeing sound and loosening muscle noises.

Stretching the tongue

Stick the tongue out of the mouth and waggle the tongue rapidly as you make fast "la-la-la-la-la-la-" sounds. Stretch the tongue by sticking it out in all directions, left, right, up, down, straight out. Talk with your tongue while sticking it out of your mouth. Then slowly bring the tongue back into the mouth, as you continue talking.

Howdie partner

Move your face around, imagine you are chewing tobacco or gum, yawn, grin, pout, kiss, and whatever else you can think of.

Dirty rat

Dirty rat is a lips exercise. Curl up your top lip and try to touch your nose with your upper lip and say with your voice "You're a dirty rat, I'm gonna get you" (à la "The Itchy and Scratchy" cartoon). Drop your lower jaw and lip as you change register by saying the US *Family Feud* TV show catch line, "and the survey says: bahm, bahm" as you drop open the lower jaw. Repeat several times.

Derek Nimmo

A vertical and horizontal yawn stretch exercise. One at a time, exaggerate and stretch the mouth open both vertically and then horizontally. Stretch your arms both upwards and across your body sideways, along with the mouth stretching exercise; as you count to ten. Count the numbers from 1 to 10 with an exaggeration – like the British actor Derek Nimmo, who always spoke with his mouth wide open. Then repeat counting the numbers in Nimmo style from 1 to 6, then 1 to 4, then 1 to 2, and then just 1, enunciating the remaining numbers in a normal, but well-articulated way.

Soft palate

Lift up your tongue and put the tip of your tongue right behind your top front teeth, inside your mouth, onto the soft palate. Keep the tip of the tongue in this position and try to stretch the body of the tongue out the front of your mouth. Similar to a sail cloth filled with wind blowing from the inside of your mouth. With the tip of your tongue on your soft palate, say the following letter sounds: *n g* followed by a short *la*. Repeat. Say *b*, *g*, *d*, *t* as short sounds. Say the following letters of the alphabet with increasing speed: *b g d – b g d – b g d, d g b – d g b – d g b, dbg – dbg – dbg* and *gdb – gdb*.

The shoulder lift

Lift your shoulders up towards your ears. Hold them up there for a moment, then drop them down again. Then repeat. Then, lift your shoulders up and drop them forward, then lift your shoulders up and drop them back to centre, then lift your shoulders up and drop then back. Move between the three, lifting and dropping the shoulders as you go forward, centre, back, centre, forward, centre, back, centre, forward, etc. When you lift and drop, try not to sway your body or back, and let your arms go wherever they want to drop to.

Stretch neck muscles

Tilt the head to the left, towards your left shoulder, and hold it there. Then put your left hand onto your right ear and hold it there. Then tilt the head slowly towards the floor and then towards the ceiling guided by the hand. Then repeat the exercise to the right. Make sure that you *tilt* the head and neck up and down and don't twist it. Then, put your hands behind the back of the head and stretch your elbows down towards the floor one by one. Gently move your elbows downwards as you stretch around the back of the neck. Never twist or force the neck.

Spinal roll

With knees bent, roll the spine, vertebra by vertebra, by first gently folding your chin and head forward, then your whole body until you are standing doubled over in a comfortable position. Reverse the process just as gently and slowly.

Peach picking

Peach picking is an exercise to help you teach yourself to get breath into particular parts of the body and to learn to control your breath and build your capacity to hold breath in the body. Imagine you are picking peaches and putting them in a basket in front of you. With an open mouth and slight smile, wait for the breath to drop in through the mouth, then reach up with your arm and pick a peach and drop it in the basket. Wait to breathe again and then do the same with the other arm. Then add sound. With every peach going into the basket let the air out with a sigh. Pick a peach with $100 attached to it and match it with your sigh. Find a peach with tickets to your favourite holiday destination and sigh accordingly. Pick a peach, stomp and sound like a sumo wrestler and throw salt into the ring. Always try to breathe into your back and diaphragm when doing the exercises.

Dr. Who

Dr. Who is an exercise that helps you start to connect breath with sound and build internal breathing. Lying on the floor with your eyes closed, let the breath fill your lower abdomen, (imagine filling a tyre, a bucket going down a well, water over a waterfall, breath coming down your spine, filling up your belly and into your back), and on the outbreath sigh "haaa", then "horr", then "who", then combine the three sounds in the one out-breath. Then, put your hands against your lower ribs, just up from your bum and try to breathe into the backs of your hands. In essence, you are lying on the palms or backs of your hands. Then add the three sounds, "haaa","horr", "who". Then combine the three sounds in the one out-breath. Teach yourself to have clear, deep, freeing sounds, supported by breath.

> ### *Learning Point Number Six*
> - Never underestimate the importance of voice training – educate yourself and work on it.
> - Work on your posture too.

Chakra work

Chakra work helps you get in touch with your feelings, which is important for all actors. It is like putting your filing system in order or defragmenting your computer's hard drive. It is spiritual, metaphysical and cleansing in nature.

The word chakra, which derives from Sanskrit, means "wheel" or "disk", and is a concept that dates from Ancient India. The chakras are believed to be wheel-like centres of energy located at seven specific points on the body.

The seven chakras are, from the base of the body upwards:

- Root or base chakra
- Sacral chakra
- Solar plexus chakra
- Heart chakra
- Throat chakra
- Third eye chakra
- Crown chakra

When you do chakra work, it is important that you work through each chakra in the body from the root chakra upwards. This helps you align your body in a metaphysical and energetic way (some even say, in a spiritual and/or healing way).

Most importantly for the actor, if you breathe through your chakras, you are more likely to find it easier to connect with your script's text. This is so because you are getting in touch with the inner you. Your past. Your emotions. Your spiritual centre. And using this subconsciously to your advantage as you act. See the breath exercises below.

An aside: whenever I work with a student – and my students nowadays sometimes include CEOs, teachers, doctors and even sports players working in the media – I often experience that the chakra work helps that person, like actors, get in touch with who they are. This increases their capacities to grow and be much more powerful as a performer.

Chakra alignment work is *core work* for the actor because it develops the inner person *in him or herself*. It also helps the actor find the inner goings-on and motivations of *the character* that they are creating or playing.

Above: Paul with actors in the AIDA school in Hollywood, circa 2008, working on chakra and emotional connection.

This is so because chakra teachers talk about *blockages* that could exist in certain chakra areas of performers.

For example, your voice may not seem quite right. You may have very little power with your voice. By doing chakra alignment work with breathing into the fifth chakra (your throat chakra), you may discover

Chapter 4 | 89

with the help of your mind, that you have a past experience where you did not speak up. By focusing energy and breathing into clearing this area of the body, you may release a blockage from your throat, and as a consequence, alter and strengthen your voice.

An aside: A psychologist and a linguist have told me that our voices are very much influenced by things that happened to us in the past, as our voices are linked to our minds and our bodies.

Or take another example of chakra clearing work: in the past, you may have been hurt when you broke up with a partner; maybe they dumped you all of a sudden. You felt this really strongly at the time, in the gut area of your body. By doing third and fourth chakra work you could clear that blockage.

I have assisted the release of blockages from many hundreds of people in my classes. Over the years I have received dozens of thank you cards and compliments from students and students' family members, as well as partners, for helping the student clear blockages with chakra and emotional exercises. I don't ask the student what the blockages are. Or how they should do the work; I simply guide them. I am the conduit.

Chakra breath exercises

Breathing through your chakras will help you get in touch with the emotions required for your character and text.

When I worked as an actor and I needed to get emotional, I would simply drop the breath as far into my body as possible and sometimes attach an emotional recall in my mind, (something that would make me feel sad), and then I would get emotional and soon tearful. This is called *crying on cue*.

To do the chakra breath exercises: sit, or preferably, stand comfortably. Have your mouth open, slight smile and drop the breath down into the body.

Below is the chakra system in its point form.

Move through the chakra areas one at a time with breath. Feel you are breathing into each chakra point from the 1st (base) chakra, which is associated with the sound *oo*, to the 7th (crown) chakra, which is associated with the sound *Ii*, one by one. *Once you have the breath there, make the sound as listed in this order, beginning with oo.*

1st chakra **oo** *(Start here)*

2nd chakra **Oh**

3rd chakra **Or**

4th chakra **Ar**

5th chakra **Ah**

6th chakra **Ee**

7th chakra **Ii**

Emotional exercises

Emotional exercises encourage you to be emotionally ready as an actor. If you need to cry, or look like you are about to cry, you can achieve this because of your training.

I suggest you do the following six emotional exercises. They will aid you on your journey to help you connect your breath, thoughts, images and voice.

Do the breath and voice work first, followed by the chakra alignment work, and then stand in a neutral position with hips, head and shoulders in alignment, looking straight ahead. Now, breathe down into your base chakra. This is your genital area.

Do the six exercises described below, first for a while with your eyes closed. After you have been doing the exercises for a few weeks, you can do them with your eyes open if you wish.

These exercises are very powerful if done correctly. Do them in a quiet place and with no interruptions. Allow a minute between each one and, if your eyes were closed, open your eyes between each exercise.

Above: An AIDA actor doing the emotional exercises in Hollywood in 2007.

The images are the most important thing for you to see in your mind's eye when doing these exercises. What images do I choose, you might ask? You decide. Choose them from your life, but keep them to yourself. Have a box of tissues handy and allow yourself to be emotionally affected by how you feel.

When doing these exercises, literally put your fingers on your genital area. This will help you focus on breathing deep down into the body. Then go through the following exercises for approximately two minutes each.

Here are the six exercises, introduced one by one.

1. **Please come back.** Think of someone you want to call back from your life and imagine calling them back. When the image is really strong in your mind, put your hands out in front of you and call them back, saying, *"Please come back".*

2. **Get away.** Think of someone who has hurt you in the past. When the image is really strong in your mind, push the hands out in front of you in an abrupt manner and feel free to add volume to this one as you say, *"Get away",* and push the hands out.

3. **Please hold me.** Think of someone you want to be held by and, when the image is really strong in your mind, put the hands up across the chest and utter the words *"Please hold me".*

4. **Mine, I take.** Think of something you really want. This could be an Oscar or being a series regular or guest starring or recurring role, or even a burger and fries. When the image is really strong in your mind, reach out with one hand as if grabbing what you want and say, *"Mine, I take".*

5. **Mine, I give.** Imagine giving something to someone. You must know who it is you are giving it to and what you're giving. When the image is really strong in your mind, lift the hands up, put them across your chest and then open them up with your palms facing upward, as you say, *"Mine, I give".*

6. **Goodbye.** Think of somebody that you haven't seen since you said goodbye to them for the last time. When the image is really strong in your mind, lift one hand up and wave goodbye to them as you say, *"Goodbye".*

Don't commence until you connect with the image. Open your eyes between each exercise and shake that image out of your mind and body lightly.

In closing, some very smart people, including doctors of drama, have done their thesis and/or written papers and books at universities on the importance and power of breath. This is one of the things you are doing with these emotional exercises. You are connecting breath, thought, image and voice.

If you are a teenager, a parent of a teenager, or a child reading this book, it may be challenging for you to read that this teacher wants the actor to put their fingers on their genital area, their pubic bone or pubic hair areas, as a part of learning how to breathe deeply down into the body and to breathe into their root chakra. As a father of two children myself, I can understand that challenge. I never put my hands down on the genital area/pubic bone/pubic hair area of any student. I simply guide the student verbally into doing the exercises. I can assure you that there are many teachers worldwide teaching breath this way and have been doing it for a long time. As already stated, it was first taught to me at University in 1989.

A disclaimer: Do not do this deep breath work, or the chakra and emotional exercises, if you feel that you may or will become emotionally or psychologically challenged or unstable by doing so. Instead, do the work with a teacher. If you do go ahead by yourself, I shall not be liable for any ill effects incurred. I feel the need to say this as this is my first book and I have not had any of my students do this work without my guidance.

Learning Point Number Seven

- Chakra work and emotional exercise work will prepare you for any emotion that you need to connect to.
- This work will also help you connect with your own feelings and clear blockages that you might have.
- This work plays an integral role in helping you get to know who you are.

Australian techniques: Dropping In The Text

I teach five acting techniques.

Dropping In The Text is an Australian technique that I was taught and later developed by myself. Of all my techniques, I teach it the most.

The technique was initially taught to me by David Latham in Melbourne in the 1990s. David told me that aspects of it were taught to him by teachers Mike Alfreds, Leonard Meenach and Kristin Linklater.

Dropping In The Text means dropping the words of the script on which you are about to work into the body. It could be either your text from a monologue or from a scene, script or play.

Like the breath work that gets the breath down into the body and the emotional exercises that work on getting us connected with ourselves, Dropping In The Text also helps us connect, this time with text.

As a consequence, it dovetails beautifully with the aforementioned exercises because it is also taking things into the mind and body. It is kind of mind, body and spirit thinking.

Doing this technique gives you a sense of *ownership* with the text. It creates positive cell memory. The exercises are also very spiritual in nature. The words of scripts connect deeply within you. This is profound stuff indeed.

The preliminary work for Dropping In The Text is as follows:

- Break the text down into **beats**.

A beat is one section of text that you think has the same thought or action running through it. A change of thought definitely indicates a beat change. Punctuation also gives you a very good indication of a beat change (although not always). For example, a full stop (called *period* in the USA), question mark, colon, semi-colon and exclamation mark are all changes of beat.

You make the decision if you want a beat change if the line has a comma. On your script, add a beat mark, which looks like this: / *(in computer command language – a forward slash).*

An aside: Please only break *your text* into beats. If you are doing a scene in which there are two or more people in it, you only do the work on your text. Not the other person's text. This is because you won't be saying the other person's words.

- Then, give each beat an **action**. Write the action word above your printed script beat.

An action is a verb that is hard to achieve, and is preceded by the word "to". Hence, a doing word. On pages 203 and 204, I've given you an example of a script marked with beats and actions. On pages 206 and 207, I have also given you pages listing both *Action* words and *Wants* to use. I use these in my school because they will make it easier for you to attach to your work to do these exercises.

As an actor, I liked to choose provocative actions when I performed with the technique. But you decide which ones you want to use.

Dropping In The Text: The layering stages

There are six layers of work relating to Dropping In The Text.

The routine to adhere to for layers 1, 2, 3 and 4 is as follows:

Sit comfortably in a chair. Do not cross arms or legs. Your body language is open. You have your mouth open, a slight smile, and you breathe down into your root chakra. Basically, as far down into the body as you can. Please have no phone or television on. Make sure you are not eating or being distracted in any way.

Layer 1

This layer is called **the actions of the text.** Repeat the following four steps for each beat change.

I call this routine *the format*.

1. **Imagine** saying the words of the first beat with the action word in your mind. For example, "Here's what I know", is the first beat. That is, the text from the start of the monologue, up until the first beat change of the script that I have chosen here. The action word I have chosen here is "to scold".

2. **Whisper** the words of the first beat to yourself. Whisper it three different ways with the action word in your mind, "to scold".

3. **Say** the words of the first beat aloud. Thinking of the action word "to scold". Say the words three different ways.

4. **Stand up out of the chair and say** the words of the first beat of the text aloud, with the action word "to scold" in your mind. Also do this three different ways.

Rules for the above: you do not go onto the next stage of any of the beats until you feel totally satisfied with your concentration and the way you have imagined it, whispered it, said it and stood up and said it. What you are trying to do is connect with your text. Do the same format for each beat.

This method ensures you take the work within the body and are happy about it.

An aside: this technique also helps you to learn the lines quickly without even trying!

After you have finished working on the monologue or the work in that session, stand up and read the dialogue off the script aloud. Read it once and try to stay connected with what you have just said. But focus only on *saying* the text. Do not try to act or perform it; just try to connect with the text.

Another aside: this layering work is a laborious task for some people. But it will work.

Allow plenty of time after each layer for your mind, body and soul to absorb the work. At least four hours, but preferably overnight. Also, do not read text aloud that you have not dropped into the body with the first layer. Also, do not practise performing the piece in the car or for friends or in bed at night. Trust the layering system.

Actors are often way too keen to want to jump straight into some type of performance. Please don't. Take your time.

To help your three ways be different when you are *whispering*, *saying* and *standing and saying*, you have the following vocal areas at your disposal:

- Pitch
- Pace
- Pausing
- Tone (flavour)
- Volume

Layer 2

This layer is called **Dropping In The Text by itself. Thinking of the meaning of the words/lines of the text.**

What do the lines mean to you? What do the words mean? What is being said? Dissect each beat. Be pedantic and enjoy the process. For this layer please do *not* think of the actions that you used for layer 1. But do repeat the *format* that you did for layer 1.

Sit comfortably in a chair. Do not cross arms or legs. Mouth open, slight smile and breathe down into your chakra system points or as deep into your body as you can. Repeat the following four format steps for each beat change.

The format:

- **Imagine** saying the text. For example, "Here's what I know" is the first beat.
- **Whisper** the text to yourself. Repeating the same beat line as above. Whisper the text three different ways.
- **Say** the line of the text aloud. Say the text three different ways.
- **Stand up out of the chair and say** the line of the text aloud. Say the text three different ways.

Do this for all beats, one by one. After you have finished working on the monologue or the work in that session, stand and read the dialogue off the script once and try to stay connected with what you have just said. But focus only on saying the text.

Also, do not read aloud text you have not dropped into the body. Do not practise doing the piece in the car or for friends or in bed at night. Trust the layering system.

Then after again waiting four to twenty-four hours, do layer 3 following the same format.

Layer 3

This layer is called **personalising the text**.

For this layer, again, please do *not* think of the actions that you used for layer 1. But do repeat the format that you did for layer 1 and 2 – see below.

This is the layer where you get to think of your past. Something that has happened in your life that you can relate to the text. This layer is the most like Stanislavski's technique of *emotional recall*. This is so because you are thinking of something from your own life experiences that you can relate to the scene.

Note: If you cannot relate to it personally, then and only then, use Stanislavski's *magical if*. Which means, *if* that had happened to you, how would you feel?

To help you, it is OK for you to think of the text *as a whole* to help you understand the small sections that you have broken the script down into. For example, words, such as, "He" or "I said", could be a beat. So, if you look at the words in context or look at the whole text, you will be able to personalise it better.

The format:

- **Imagine** saying the text. For example, "Here's what I know" is the first beat.
- **Whisper** the text to yourself. Repeating the same beat line as above. Whisper the text three different ways.
- **Say** the line of the text aloud. Say the text three different ways.
- **Stand up out of the chair and say** the line of the text aloud. Say the text three different ways.

Repeat this for all beats, one by one. After you have finished working on the monologue or the work in that session, stand and read the dialogue off the script once and try to stay connected with what you have just said. But focus only on saying the text.

Also, do not read aloud text you have not dropped into the body. Do not practise doing the piece in the car or for friends or in bed at night. Trust the layering system. Then after, again waiting four to twenty-four hours, do layer 4.

Layer 4

This layer is called **physicalising the words and images in space.**

This is like putting the words out onto a whiteboard or a black wall; like in space.

See the words (and images, if they appear for you), beat by beat, as you drop the words into the body. Like on a clear whiteboard or black wall. Think to yourself: *look at the words I am saying.*

Actors often say to me that they see images with the text or they see the computer serif typeface, like Times New Roman or Courier New; all this is good and will help you.

If, for some reason, you don't see the text from the beat, like it is written on a wall, get up and walk over and pretend to hand write the words of that beat, such as "Here's what I know" on the wall, then go back and sit down.

For this layer, again do *not* think of the actions that you used for layer 1. But do repeat the format that you did for layers 1, 2 and 3. That is: the format.

- **Imagine** saying the text. For example, "Here's what I know" is the first beat.
- **Whisper** the text to yourself. Repeating the same beat line as above.
- **Say** the line of the text aloud.
- **Stand up out of the chair and say** the line of the text aloud.

Repeat this for all beats, one by one. After you have finished working on the monologue or the work in that session, stand and read the dialogue off the script once and try to stay connected with what you have just said. But focus only on saying the text.

Also, do not read aloud text you have not dropped into the body. Do not practise doing the piece in the car or for friends or in bed at night.

Again, trust the layering system.

Layers 5 and 6 are performance layers.

You no longer sit in the chair with open body language. You now stand up with open body language and perform the scene or monologue and receive direction from a teacher or coach.

Layer 5

This layer is called **dealing with wants.**

With guidance, preferably from your teacher, the direction given is now going to focus on your character's *wants*; their subtext. Only work with one want at a time. But I suggest you choose a few different wants to work with. Write, say, *three* different wants across the top of the script. This helps give your performance variety. Then work through each want, one at a time.

For guidance, see the list of *Wants*, on page 207.

Wants are the overall objective of the piece. Make them separate from the text, hard to achieve and *from*, or, you are doing it *to*, the person opposite you in the scene. Or from the audience, or from yourself, if doing a soliloquy.

Then act the scene thinking of the want. Then do it again choosing and thinking of another want. Do this three times, each time with a different want.

Layer 6

This layer is called **changing your points of concentration.**

This layer is designed to take you out of your comfort zone. It will get you to think of different and variable circumstances.

While performing, preferably with a teachers' guidance, you could think: "You hate your father" or "Your lover is just outside the door" or "You are about to collapse from exhaustion".

So, act the scene thinking of the given point of concentration. Then do it again with a different point of concentration. Do this three times, each time with a different point of concentration.

When you get used to doing it, you will notice that you can still connect with your text as you perform.

The aim of the technique

The overall aim of this technique is to take the work into the body and for you to connect with it. As said, preferably work with a teacher or acting coach on layers 5 and 6 as this will help you discover new things and take you out of your comfort zone.

An apt metaphor for you to think of when doing these layers is this: a casting director or a director is adjusting your performance and/or character in different ways. This is apt because once the work is in the body, the actor is in a position to play and be directed. This is really important as both casting directors and directors like to give actors direction and like it when you do what they want.

With the work inside the body, the actor is then in a position to be guided and directed to do whatever they want, and yet, most importantly, still connect with their text; even emotionally. This is empowering. This helps you make impact as you perform.

Should you always have subtext or a point of concentration going with your work? No, not necessarily. The main reasons that I teach subtext and points of concentration is to stretch you as an actor and also prepare you to be versatile and be ready and capable to take direction in auditions and on set or stage.

Casting directors and directors love it if the actor does as they ask. Because they can see that the actor is flexible, and instead of being rigid or stuck in any set way, they will rise to the occasion and alter their performance to suit the direction that they were given.

The last thing a casting director or a director wants to see is giving direction to an actor who does the same thing again. The same way. You may know that this is a *pet peeve* of casting directors, casting associates and directors alike. Why is it so? Because many actors simply give the same or a very similar performance once directed, including what they physically do with their bodies. If you don't alter your performance when given direction, you will not make a good impression with the casting director.

The breath and voice work and the Dropping In The Text work that I teach is a part of what I like to call foundation work. I would like you to think that it is like the concrete stumps (cornerstone, for Americans) of a house. This seems an apt analogy.

An aside: How many layers of Dropping In The Text should you do before an audition? The answer is, as many as you can in the time frame permitted, prior to going to the audition.

> ### *Learning Point Number Eight*
> - The Dropping In The Text technique will help you connect with the words and images that you will say.
> - You will always be flexible in performance and you will also be able to be directed easily.
> - The consequences are, you perform stronger and are able to be directed.

Above top: Paul and interpreter Jani Wang with the students at Geely University in Beijing, China, in 2010. Above bottom: Geely University students are listening to a lecture, given by Paul as they hold AIDA handouts.

Below: Paul teaching at Jikei International Acting School in Tokyo, Japan, in 2017.

Above: Paul teaching in Stone Wings Acting School in Tokyo in 2018.

Listening

Listening is one of the best ways to notice the differences between a professional actor and an amateur actor. Professional actors *really* listen. Amateur actors wait for their cue. What do you do?

I say to actors, acting begins with two words – breath and listening. Where do you breathe to and from in the body, and how well do you listen?

There are many different kinds of listening. There is listening for what you want in a scene. There is listening for the sounds that are coming out at you from others. There is listening for subtle changes in tone, pitch, volume and even pauses. There is listening when being in a state of anticipation. There is listening *acting* because you have to pretend that you do not know the lines that are coming out at you, and there is listening to your own voice and sounds.

Unfortunately, there is also choosing to listen to the critic or voice in your head or the critic that sits on your shoulder. More on this soon.

Try to do as much "other person" listening as possible. Most importantly, simply listen. If you do, and you are in front of a camera, you will see that your eyes boggle or dance or move slightly. Not everybody's eyes dance or boggle or move a little when they are listening; but most people's do. The camera and in turn the audience subconsciously love this.

Movie stars are generally all very good listeners.

An aside: USA actor Anne Heche has *eyes that boggle and dance* more than any other actors' eyes that I have seen on screen. The amazingly brilliant British actress Sally Hawkins comes a close second.

I do a few different listening exercises in my classes. Below are some things that you can do to help you improve your listening:

- Sit or stand still. Close your eyes and listen to the sounds in the room. Listen to the sounds outside the room. Try to identify and distinguish between the sounds
- When spoken to, repeat some things that were said to you back to the other person
- Think, "What did that person just say to me?" after you have finished a conversation and walked away from them

Anticipation

Anticipation is a wonderful state to be in as an actor because we like looking at people in this state. I teach it.

Life is an improvisation, isn't it? This is because, generally, we do not know what will be said or done to us at any given moment. We are consequently, in life, constantly in a state of anticipation.

Our face, eyes, ears and attention are generally all pointing in the direction of the person who is talking to us. Put yourself in this state of mind as much as you can as an actor.

You can practise being in a state of anticipation by listening and by doing this exercise: when looking at someone talking to you, just as they start talking, quickly say to yourself, "What are they going to say or do next?" Then listen!

This will help your listening skills and help you be much more spontaneous with your responses. You will be much more *in the moment* both verbally and non-verbally and consequently much more watchable as an actor.

> ## *Learning Point Number Nine*
> - Listen like a hawk!
> - Put your mind, body and soul into a state of anticipation.
> - Be excited and open to hear or see what is going to happen next.

Letting it land

In life, did you hear what was said to you? We hope you did. After all, communication in life is an improvisation, isn't it? Because, as said, we don't know what is going to be said to us next.

When acting, it is absolutely vital that when people say things to you, you *really* hear it. Let it affect you and then respond according to how your character would in a scene.

I call this *letting it land.* This may sound simple in theory, but a lot of actors do not do this enough. If you run with the concept that the number one thing that we watch when watching actors in a camera mid-shot, or any other close-up shot, is *the eyes*, then we need to see that you are being affected *in the eyes*. Or at least on the face.

I ask you to consider this: if you were to go to the hairdressers and spend $150 on your hair (and you liked it), and then you go home to your partner, best friend or parent, and have them say, "What the hell have you done with your hair, it looks terrible". Then you would be affected by what is said to you.

Well, the same goes for acting. Some actors tend to generally only respond to extreme, dramatic circumstances, such as: I am going to hit you; I have cancer; I have Covid; or I slept with your partner.

In life, we are constantly moved and touched and emotionally affected, and we generally respond accordingly. We respond to what is said to us in life, in all circumstances. Therefore, the good actor must respond in a scene based on his character and the story in the same way. *Letting it land* will help this.

In addition, the use and sound of someone else's voice and the use of their body language are signs that need to be acknowledged and responded to.

For example, in life if you are talking to someone and they raise their voice, you generally raise your voice too. If the tone of their voice becomes comforting and soft, yours does too. If they lean over and put their elbow on the table while talking to you over a cup of coffee, well, after a short period of time, you are most likely going to do the same thing. You will mirror them.

Unfortunately, these verbal and non-verbal actions, or ways of behaviour, are often missed by some actors.

In support of this I would like to add – and please excuse the generalisation – that lots of actors are prone to looking at the floor and anywhere else but at the other person when performing in a scene.

If you are one of those actors, what you have to do is *let it land*. You have to make the choice to do the following: watch the other actor/s, hear it, take it in, be observant in all ways and respond verbally and non-verbally to what is given to you. Here are the key elements to help you achieve this goal:

- Look the other actor (or reader, or casting director) in the eye before the scene begins. Observe their body language and the way they are looking at you
- Listen like a hawk. Actors who don't listen are dead in the water and will never make it

- Go for your want or your opinion or your attitude or point of concentration (I elaborate on these points later in the book)
- Begin the scene *with* the other person and be affected by everything that is said to you and that is done to you through their body language and the tone, flavour, pitch and volume of their voice

An aside: this does not mean take thirty seconds to respond to every line. Actors have to earn a pause in a scene. Wherever there is a scene where you can drive a truck through the pause, the scene is too slow. But if you pay special attention with your eyes and ears, you'll be off to a good start and most likely will respond naturally.

- Continue going for your want or opinion or attitude or point of concentration until the end of the scene

Best of luck. Let it land.

Control

Should we be in control? This is a contentious topic.

Actors should absolutely have a *sense* of what they are trying/wanting to do and where they want to go with their work. But they should not try to control everything that they are doing, once the scene starts.

I see actors trying to control what they are doing so much that they become stuck inside their own heads and are not available to receive the *in the moment* gems that could come up in one of the following ways:

- The other person says or does something different
- There's a loud noise or something falls on the floor, which could and should be incorporated into the work or scene; but it is ignored by the actor
- The actor has a glazed look over their eyes, because they are sitting on their own shoulder watching their work and not really listening, or they are directing themselves from within their own

mind because they are controlling or trying to control what is going on

Unfortunately, I've seen many actors over the years who should be writers, directors, producers or teachers, and not actors, because of their willingness to control what is going on as it is going on. Don't do it. Get out of your own head and try not to control things. Let the director, casting director or teacher direct the work. You act.

AIDA students performing with the neutral mask – Hollywood, LA, USA.

Chapter 5
International theorists: Four other techniques that I teach

Teacher training of the actor should be very rich, very diverse, full of versatility, full of challenges and above all, full of honesty.

In addition to the Australian techniques discussed in the previous chapter, I also incorporate international theorists into my teaching. Five international theorists have had the strongest influence on my coaching. Four of them have their own acting technique. Some aspects of these techniques are taught at schools in Australia and in other parts of the world. They are: Jerry Grotowski from Poland, Rudolf Laban from Hungary, Bertolt Brecht from Germany and Constantine Stanislavski from Russia. Some of the other exercises I teach are from Jacques Lecoq from France.

There are many books that have been written on these great people. So I will not write too much about them here. What I will do, though, is talk about how these four theorists' versatile and influential acting techniques, and in Jacques Lecoq's case – his exercises for actors – all improve the actor's work.

To begin with, Grotowski, Laban and the Neutral Mask work of Jacques Lecoq all focus on encouraging the actor to use their body – preferably every muscle in their body to its greatest capacity. Of course, they also challenge the actor's mind, but the use of the body is the main focus.

Jerzy Grotowski

Grotowski calls his theatre *a laboratory*. He gets his actors to wear very little clothing, usually a lap lap (a waist cloth or loin cloth), or he clothes his students all in black.

An aside: Students in my AIDA school in the USA between 2002 and 2011 were all uniformed in black.

Grotowski calls his audience *spectators* and asks his actors to make a total *sacrifice* of themselves towards their craft and their audience. Grotowski's work is very physical. It is invigorating both for the actor to perform and for the audience to watch.

Grotowski's work improves the actor's work because it helps them become aware that they can use every muscle in their bodies. The work searches for the truth from their bodies. The work wants them to be creative and not give the audience the stereotype.

When I teach Grotowski's work, I read the warm-up exercises straight from his book, *Towards a Poor Theatre*. I ask actors to interpret what Grotowski is asking the actor to do; in their own way. I simply ask for freedom of expression and tell them, "There is no wrong way of doing an exercise". Actors love it when I say that to them. I then improvise with the actors, getting them to play different animals in several ways. I then introduce script.

Grotowski's work wants actors to think of themselves as animals and to think *what type of animal* relates to the character that they are playing and how can they bring out the *animalistic* qualities in everything that they do as a part of their preparation.

It is through this rawness, this openness, this commitment, both physically and vocally, that one challenges, stretches and awakens the actor's body. It is the actor's *giving* of their body and the *focus* of their energy into their work that is intense, draining and yet very rewarding. The actor feels much more relaxed, freer and committed to the expression of their work. This type of physical work thus personifies an actor's commitment to their craft.

If you work on an audition scene, then do a Grotowski class, and then go back to the same scene, even if it is for a television audition, the actor will produce a much more open, more committed, less stereotypical performance, with the voice and with the body.

I suggest you get a copy of Grotowski's book, *Towards a Poor Theatre*, and start doing his exercises.

Rudolph Laban

Hungarian dancer and choreographer Rudolf Laban was a pioneer of modern dance. He created a technique that made actors become aware of things such as *Space* and *Time*. That is, what are the distances between actors and how could one use those distances to their advantage?

Laban is also known for BESS: Body, Effort, Shape, Space. Laban's BESS technique for actors explores the body in space, the different types of commitment we can use, the shapes we can create and the influences we can have on ourselves, our fellow actors and the audience; all with the body.

Laban also created a list of *working actions* in which actors can break their script down into what he called *beats*.

An aside: interestingly, as already explained, my Australian techniques also uses *beats*.

I work mainly with Laban's *working actions* in class. Working actions are a list of actions designed to give the actor a physical system to follow each time they rehearse. For example, do I *flick* my body on this line, or *glide* or *slash* my body as I deliver the next line of the text?

Laban's eight working actions are:

1. **Punch:** Strong /Direct/ Quick
2. **Slash:** Strong / Flexible / Quick
3. **Wring:** Strong/ Flexible / Sustained
4. **Press:** Strong / Direct / Sustained
5. **Float:** Light / Flexible / Sustained

6. **Glide:** Light / Direct / Sustained

7. **Dab:** Light / direct / Quick

8. **Flick:** Light / Flex / Quick

The actor uses their own interpretation of what each action means to them. For each action, Laban adds particular movement "paces", as listed above. Each movement pace affects the way in which the actor will move. For example, they are moving: strong or light, flexible or direct, quick or sustained.

Actors experience these *verbal* body movements to make sure the body has the sensation; in other words, they are linking the mind and body memory. Actors practise and rehearse these movements so they become familiar with them.

Laban's acting technique work, originating from his dance theories, is good for actors because the actor is able to use their mind and body almost like creating patterns. Once the student's mind remembers the working actions in sequence, the body does too; it remembers the routine, like a dancer's body remembers choreography. This type of movement is very freeing for the body. As you can imagine, it becomes extremely captivating to watch.

I love teaching Laban and I love the way it improves actors' work because it is another way of achieving free expression with the body.

Actors sometimes say to me in class, "I do not know what to do with my body". Or, "I don't know what to do with my hands". Working on Laban's techniques for actors will help you become aware of yourself in the space, your special connections with other actors, and open you up to use your body to help emphasise a point.

It is very different work from Grotowski's movement work as Grotowski work is much more primal. Whereas Laban's working actions are based on the interpretation in the mind of what *flick* or *dab* etc. mean to you. In addition, your paces – *direct, sustained* etc. – will, most likely, be very different from the next actor's. This is so because, again, it is your interpretation.

An aside: Cate Blanchett mentioned in an interview while she was in the USA, that she remembered working on, and using Laban's working actions when at acting school in Australia.

I suggest you try playing with the working actions. Break your script down into beats and put a working action on each beat and start playing around with them.

Bertolt Brecht

German playwright and director Bertolt Brecht, in later years, wrote plays that insisted actors acknowledge that they were performing, that they were simply actors in the play telling a story. Brecht eventually called the type of theatre that he liked to create and direct *epic theatre*.

Using plays that he had written or co-written Brecht directed his actors to perform his epic theatre adhering to what was eventually called an *estrangement effect* or *alienation effect* – meaning, a distancing effect.

The aim of Brecht's work was to provoke social and political change and draw its audiences' attention to social and political issues.

His theatre is often, not funny on the page, or in subject matter, but it is often very funny in execution. This is due to the *estrangement effect* of things that his actors, and the production in general, are adhering to when performing a Brecht play in his theatre.

Brecht's technique is the most external of the international theorists that I like to teach.

I call it a technique because Brecht wants all actors of his works to approach and perform his plays adhering to estrangement and alienation. In other words, Brecht's actors are asked to draw attention to the fact that they *are actors*.

If they do show emotion in a scene or it surfaces somehow in the production, they are to draw attention to the fact that they are actors and acting for the benefit of the play's main contentions.

An aside: like Grotowski, interestingly, Brecht also calls his audience *spectators*.

With Brecht's *estrangement*, the actors in Brecht theatre often talk directly to the audience. This helps break down the "fourth wall" (an imaginary wall that separates the actor from the audience) and indirectly builds a relationship between the actor and his audience. Then the actor is in a position to *pass on a message* and thereby evoke social and political change.

Some scholars credit Chinese theatre as an influence on Brecht's epic theatre. I acknowledge this and also feel that there are definite correlations between Brecht's type of theatre performance and vaudeville theatre, as performed in some countries, including the USA in the late nineteenth and early twentieth centuries.

Another aside: as Brecht lived in California for a while in the 1930s, perhaps Brechtian theatre helped develop the origins of the stand-up comic too?

Brecht's approach to acting improves an actor's work because it allows the actor to let go, laugh at themselves and have fun. Actors generally let go and become very passionate about Brecht's political and social points.

Actors have to learn some different things when performing Brecht style, such as: maintaining eye contact with the audience, mocking theatrical conventions by, for example, drawing attention to the stage lights or the music or reading the stage directions from the play.

Brecht's work helps build the actor's confidence because it helps them see the effect that their work is having directly on the audience.

The types of actors listed below will thrive when performing Brecht's style of acting using the *estrangement effect:*

- The comic actor
- The stand-up comic
- The actor who is good at imitating
- The actor who loves an audience

In support of this, the actor who enjoys provoking an audience into social and political change will also love the effects of Brecht's acting technique and the messages through his plays.

Here are a few tips on performing Brecht's style of acting:

- Enter the stage holding a sign with your full name stating you are an actor playing a part in a play
- Look directly into the audience's eyes and interact with them with the dialogue
- Try not to get emotionally involved in what you are saying. However, if you start to get emotional, hold up a sign saying, "I am just an actor, don't be fooled". Then hold up another sign saying, "But what do you think of the political or social issue that I am addressing here?"
- Enter a scene holding a card or poster, or use some other theatrical device, letting the audience know that you are advocating a particular viewpoint
- Mock your costume or props
- Use tacky or easily seen theatrical conventions. For example, music that comes from a CD player that the audience can see
- Caricature your character and move between seriousness and mockery of your character's cause

Above top pic: Drama Department assistant and Jack Fu are with Paul in front of the drama building at Geely University in Beijing. AIDA USA student Jani Wang, who was the translator on the teaching tour, and who has been trained by Paul, has 24 IMDB credits as of June, 2022.

Above bottom pic: Paul with Professor Mr. Qin Jiefeng, Vice President, Hainan University-Sanya College in Hainan, China, along with interpreter Jani Wang and businessman Jack (Jian) Fu.

Konstantin Stanislavski

Everything that grows out of the ground has roots. The roots of twentieth and even twenty-first-century acting and actor training undoubtedly come from this most influential man – Russian, Konstantin Stanislavski.

Many actors in training classes and many schools in the USA today use programs that are some sort of adaptation of Stanislavski's work. Whether it is Adler, Hagen, Meisner or Strasberg, they're all adaptations from Stanislavski. Many people also connect the likes of Morris, Fine, Chubbuck and others to Stanislavski too.

My Australian training and some of what I teach also incorporates work from Stanislavski. For example, I like to train actors to go for their *want*. I like actors to be emotionally connected with their work and I like actors to be able to access all of their body and all of their voice, including their use of breath, with their want. These things all have correlations with some of Stanislavski's teachings.

Actors that play *subtext* and hopefully *emotionally connect* with their work and use their breath and voice in conjunction with their work, are often much more honest and real then those who do not.

Emotional recall, for example, is a vital tool for the actor. I believe it is a positive thing for the actor to use their own emotions from their past experiences in life, in with their work – not to tell anyone what they are, but feel free to use them.

I agree with Stanislavski that emotional recall is fruitful and can assist the actor to get to where they need to be emotionally. That is, to help them connect with what they are saying and doing.

As said already, I encourage this emotional work to be done, *internally* without the actor having to tell the teacher the emotional recall that they are using. I think it is better this way, rather than the student telling a teacher of their own personal emotional past.

Stanislavski's technique improves the actor's work because it demands that they have an *internal mind process* to follow and to help them make decisions.

Stanislavski asks you to use your own *experiences* for motivation to help you connect with what you are saying and doing; and because it frees you up to also think of the magical *if*.

I teach ways to help actors connect to their work, but if they can't, the *magical if* can help you. Using the magical *if* means asking yourself *if* that happened to me or *if* I had to do that, what would I do? It is simple really. Suspend your belief and think of the *magical if*, one hundred percent.

If you have heard of the following words, or, if you have been asked by a director or a casting director: "What does your character want?" or, "What's your character's objective?", or, "What's your character's subtext?", or, "What's your character's need?" or "What's your character's desire?" – they basically all mean the same thing – what does your character want?

Here are some exercises to help you playing *wants*:

- Watch people all day and try to guess their wants
- Practise playing different wants
- Go for your *want* verbally, or just go for it with the use of your body. Then with both. Think: how do I convey with my body what I want? How do I convey with my voice what I want?

- Emotionally recall an event that happened to you in the past. Then attach it to a scene at a particular point and do the scene again. See if it improves your work
- Imagine *if* you had killed someone the next time you play a character who has killed someone (many drama scripts have a murderer in them)

In addition, it is worth noting that by dealing with your past trauma or emotional experiences through, say, Stanislavski's emotional recall exercises, this can be a good thing in both the immediate and lifelong journey of you, the human being, working as an actor.

I believe this is so because, as discussed already, the more we know about ourselves, theoretically, the better person we will become. We will also have better relationships with others. We will definitely become a better actor, and the planet will be a better place too.

Exercises that I teach: Jacques Lecoq and the neutral mask

In Ancient Greece, performers used to wear masks and perform as a group, a chorus. One day a man stepped out of his group, and spoke. He was the first actor, and his name was *Thespis*. Hence the industry nickname of *thespians* for actors.

Theatre masks have taken many different forms over the centuries – for example, the Ancient Greek chorus masks or the *comedia dell'arte* masks worn in Italy. I wish to talk here of the *neutral masks* described by the Frenchman Jacques Lecoq in the twentieth century.

Lecoq's neutral masks are plain with no expression or hair or character face on them. They are, generally, a white or skin-coloured mask with holes for the actors' eyes, nose and mouth.

The neutral mask is a profoundly freeing tool for the actor. To begin with, the actor does not speak with the mask on and the actor's whole face is covered, apart from the eyes, the nose and the mouth.

Most actors really like working with a neutral mask on. This is because it opens them up in ways that they may never have imagined. It encourages them to express with their body in a way that is invigorating and entertaining for both themselves and their audience.

This is because the mask hides their face; even their eyes. Unless you are close to the actor, their eyes cannot be seen. This gives the actor a profound sense of freedom.

With Lecoq work, the actor's focus should not be on being entertaining or performing for a laugh. Rather it is all about expression, creativity, freedom and working in well with other actors' body language.

Similar to the truthfulness in Grotowski work, neutral mask work encourages, implores, even demands, honesty from the actor.

Many shy, introverted, passive actors come alive with expression with their bodies when wearing the neutral mask. Sometimes they become a totally changed performer with the neutral mask on their face.

I love to teach neutral mask work. It improves actors' work because of this openness, this freshness, this sense of play that the actor allows themselves to have with the neutral mask on.

Give it a try. It will demand from you a sense of giving, a sense of truth, when you put the mask on. Like me, I'm guessing that you will grow to respect the neutral mask.

What to do with the mask on? Here are some exercises you can try. Only use your body. No props. No talking.

- Paint with the utensil of your choice
- Cook anything you want
- Dance
- Perform a monologue in your mind, without speaking
- Watch other people do something
- Do something with someone else. Work out what they are doing and join in with them

As said, all without sound. Without uttering a word.

I would like to finish this section by saying this: many actors don't know how to use their bodies for affect.

I often work with Grotowski, Laban and Lecoq exercises to free them up, to try and eliminate their self-consciousness and to help them develop their movement and use of body skills; for both stage and screen.

An aside: American actress Allison Janney is marvellous at using her body on screen.

Learning Point Number Ten

- What technique works for you? Find one and use it.
- Or maybe learn a few and take bits from each, if that works better for you.
- If you feel you have a weakness in a particular area, use parts of a technique to help you.

Chapter 6
Preparing for an audition

In the performance industry there is a lot of controversy that surrounds how best an actor should approach auditioning. Should actors make decisions prior to their performance at an audition? Some teachers say no. I say yes, they should. I would like to qualify my statement here by saying this: you make decisions as a part of your preparation, then you let go of your decisions as you start the audition performance.

Knowing how to audition is very important. In the industry you hear stories all the time about how well someone can audition or not. Hence, being able to audition *well* is a vital skill. Many less talented actors book work simply because of their ability to audition well. To audition well requires two things: training and preparation.

Training, meaning training yourself to be better at auditioning. Preparation, meaning the things you need to do to prepare for each audition.

I suggest you do mock auditions in front of your family, friends and peers. You should also do mock auditions in acting classes.

While I was working as a professional actor in Melbourne and Sydney in Australia in the 1990s, a group of actors and I would all work together, on and off camera, on mock auditions. The booking rate of all of us increased because of these mock auditions.

One success story in Melbourne from these classes went like this: there was an actor in our workshop who had to respond to being beaten up in a scene at an audition for a television show called *Blue Heelers*.

The actor in the workshop received constant banter from all of the other actors in the workshop to help him get to be fearful and emotional. He went straight from our workshop to the audition. He booked the job.

He asked the casting director and then the director of that episode when he was on set, why they chose him, and they said, "Because you looked the most scared and tapped into your emotions the quickest at the audition".

What we did at our shared group workshop profoundly helped him. This is an example of audition preparation at its finest.

Above: Paul taking a break from his teaching tour in 2019 – Manhattan, New York City.

No such thing as perfection

Actors pressure themselves when they audition. Many actors seek perfection. They try to control what they are doing and worry too much about their own performance and whether or not the casting people will like their choices.

All of this pressure and worry is a waste of time. Actors need to train themselves to do the preparatory work and then learn to relax, trust their choices, let go, play and try to be in the moment, so that nothing else is distracting them. You are simply enjoying the experience, communicating what you want to do and being affected by what is said and done to you in the experience.

To be specific, you must be affected by what is said to you and how it is said to you, and by what is done to you and how it is done to you. In other words, you stay present in the scene and be ready for change. This is because in life, we don't know what people will say next, so we kind of improvise.

In life, we are not following a script. Actors must therefore leave this element of openness in their psyche, their body and their involvement in a scene in an audition.

There is no such thing as perfection anyway. It is subjective. So why bother going for it?

Enjoy yourself instead and try to remember this way of thinking when you audition next: I will go on an unknown journey in the audition.

I want you all to also know that sometimes actors actually do better work when they stop trying. This is because they let go. They take the pressure off themselves and allow themselves to actually personify things they have learnt already. Don't try so hard.

Paul Parker: What I want to do here is to link in or tap into the stuff you wrote last week because, actors, so much of your success as a professional actor, once you can basically act, and you start doing a good job with your acting (basically everyone is doing a good job with their acting; you're just working on your skills to improve and learning to stretch yourself etc.) well, so much of what you do and how to do it really well so you stand out, which includes whether you book the work or not; has to do with what's going on in your mind.

One of the topics I am addressing in the book that I am writing is self-sabotage and procrastination. This surfaces in many different ways. So, let me give you an example of how it surfaces. You prepare for an audition, you go to the audition, you're feeling pretty good about it, you're about to go in and then you're like, "Oh no, I'm not prepared enough; I'm not going to do a good job".

Or you say to yourself, "I think I've made the wrong choices and it's too late to change". Sometimes it's, "Look at all the other girls here, they're all dressed up in uniforms and I'm wearing business attire, I'm not going to get the part".

Or, "Look at all the other girls or guys, they're all so much better looking than I am". Or, "This casting director just came out and didn't even look at me before he took the other actor into the audition room, that must mean that he doesn't like me!"

I'm giving you many examples, and there are many more. What about the actor who comes in to the audition and dumps this scenario, "I've been stuck in traffic for so and so hours", or the actor who comes in and dumps this scenario, "It took me forever to find parking, do you know how hard it is to find parking in your neighbourhood, I've been driving around for fifteen minutes?"

Actors, please don't ever forget that the person who sits by the front door or at the front desk will eventually, most likely, become a casting director.

That person working at a casting office, even if they're volunteering, wants to be a casting director, and eventually they will be a casting director or a casting director's assistant.

What I am giving you here are examples of actors self-sabotaging. Then you get the actors who don't even show up and procrastinate. Then you've got the actor who will go out the night before a major audition and deliberately get drunk or stay up all night and turn up to the audition late thinking, "Oh, I'm OK, a bit hung over but OK, I'm still putting my best foot forward"; but they are not.

Then you've got the actor with the internal belief that they are not good enough and that they don't deserve it. They don't deserve to get paid.

Just so you know, every actor that walks into this room, into my class, even if they're a beginner and says, "I'm here to study to become an actor", I deem them and talk to them as if they were a professional actor.

I know that just about everybody in this room is auditioning and getting work and all that sort of stuff. Which is great, as I want this for all the students in the school. As you know, I'll treat you all as professional actors.

In coming back to this point: so much of how far you're going to go and how much success you are going to have, has got a lot to do with what's going on in your head.

Let me make your work here extremely practical. Here is a practical experience of self-sabotage. I hope that this scenario does not happen too often. I heard a student ask before: "What do I do if I feel insecure about the decisions I've made based on the script". You all heard my answer on what was the best thing to do.

Well, this is how it goes: the student prepares and then gets very anxious because he thinks that he's done the wrong thing as he's sitting there waiting to go in for his audition.

He's done all his preparation, but now the pressure is on and he's feeling a bit nervous. He's right there at the audition and saying to himself, "Ah jeez, I've made the wrong decision and I should have insisted to my manager that we get the whole script", and "Oh shit, I'm dressed all differently to everybody else, and I'm unshaven and they're all shaven; I am not going to get this part, I'm wasting my time; I could have been at my part-time job today getting at least sixty dollars in tips".

This is the self-talk of actors. I've been in this business a long time . . . since 1977. I can tell you that I've seen and heard profound self-sabotage and procrastination stories from actors; including from my own mind.

Well after that introduction, let's try to find a solution, let's link back to your work last week. Last week I asked you all, and some of you can do this very quickly, to write down some of your concerns about auditioning. I asked you to get into groups, and the people that were new to this group were to tell the others of this group what some of those concerns were.

You all chewed the fat, and the more experienced of this group offered suggestions on how to do it. Let's revisit that because, with all of you, not just the ones who auditioned last week, I want to know and I want you to be comfortable with saying it, I want to know what has re-surfaced tonight.

I want to know the connection, the correlation between what you wrote down, about your concerns when you auditioned and what happened when you auditioned with me tonight. I want to know before you see your work because generally, you are never going to see your work in most instances when you audition. We talked about that before as well.

(An aside: I know that being able to see your audition work has changed a lot since this class took place.)

Obviously, you've got to be comfortable sharing it. One of the beautiful things about sharing thoughts, actors, is the obvious . . . that you will get empathy, that you will get support.

A student said a wonderful thing last week to me, for those of you who weren't here, this girl here is going on about the things that were happening with her, and things that weren't working because of this and because of that, because I was this and my hair was this, and yadda yadda yadda. She was self-sabotaging instead of thinking about the work.

So, tonight we are going to pick out the most important thing – your problem – and see if it surfaced in this simulated audition class.

We're looking for something and we will try to resolve and heal it to make the experience better. This is absolutely an open forum and not only will you get my opinion, but you are also going to get the words of your peers.

Actors, it has to be something that you are prepared and open to share with the group. Let's all go around articulating one concern and let's start here [I point to someone].

Student: I felt so self-conscious. I felt like I was thinking of everything, my hair, everything and I was afraid my decisions were not strong enough.

Paul: OK, thanks, you felt watched and you felt self-conscious/self-aware. Is this something that you feel when you normally audition? [Student nods – yes.] You do. Give us the exact specifics so we all know what to work on and how you feel when you audition.

In other words, something like "I stood out in front of the camera, I stood on the mark and I looked up and saw all of the students, who had already auditioned, staring at me that were in the room". Is that how you felt? That's what I mean, be that specific.

Student: It's about me knowing that there is a camera there and it's going to get watched later on that day and I'm being judged. Judged and scrutinised and every little move I make will get magnified.

Paul: It can be, especially if you're in a close-up. So, it was the camera, it's the after-thought of doing the work? So, what this actor is doing is stepping out of her preparation and making comments about herself before it even happens.

The first thing is, this is something very honest and dear to the heart that this actor is concerned about. So, we have to respect that and be extremely grateful that she is sharing it.

And the next thing I want to let you know is that you're not alone. Actors that step out, whether it's in a performance or in preparation or out in the hallway, well, this behaviour is common from actors.

What can we do to help this actor? Wait a moment, who else in this room feels the same? [Many hands go up.] Well, what can we do? [Students speak.] Who said be in the moment? What do you mean? You're absolutely right, if in doubt; listen! Tell yourself to re-focus. To put your energy back into the work. Listen harder.

Actors, I suggest you write down these statements that I am about to give you, memorise them, place them around yourself in your life and practise living these statements:

- Whatever I do is okay
- I will prepare the best I can in the time frame permitted
- I'm good enough and I can do well
- I will come from love and not fear

These statements will help you take the pressure off yourself. Help you stay focused and help you think positively, as opposed to negatively.

We are what we think. Create positive experiences and take the pressure off yourself. Make choices and trust them. Trust you. Does that help, actors?

All actors agreed and wrote them down. End of transcription.

My teaching of actors regarding auditioning is to prepare them and train them to audition very well. This includes to take risks. My trainings' main contention is called *empowerment*. Here is a list of things that an actor should generally do prior to, and when, auditioning:

- Have made choices and preferably be off script. Choices meaning: you have made decisions about who you are and how you feel about the people you are talking to and what you want and what is going on and what you are trying to do. Off script means: you know your lines
- Used a technique on the work
- Have done a backstory to scene and to character (as described in my scene study section on pages 240 to 243)
- Turned up early
- Been polite and friendly and grateful for being there
- Not carried baggage of, "It is about time you got me in!" into the studios
- Been one hundred percent professional. No complaining whatsoever
- Made a subtle choice of what to wear that suits the character
- If an on-camera audition, not worn white or stripes or circles or a multi-coloured shirt with patterns on it
- If on camera, asked the frame, "What camera shot am I being shot in, please?" This is so you can adjust your performance accordingly
- Tried to make connection with the casting director. Move towards them slowly when they talk to you
- Be prepared to take the scene anywhere
- Repeat aloud the direction the casting director gives you
- Stay calm and relaxed
- Thank them for getting you in

- Not ask: "When will I hear if I get the job?"

In closing, auditioning is very different in many ways to acting. In acting, the actor usually gets to a point where they let go and act; which of course, they love doing because they have gotten the job.

But in auditioning, the mind can play many tricks. The actor's insecurities could, and often do, surface because the actor is trying to get the job. The sabotage. The procrastination. The voice sitting on the actor's shoulder. All of these things could surface.

What you have to do is train yourself to think the right way. Not judge. Let go. Play. Enjoy, trust your choices and, most importantly, learn to control the inner voice, or the critic in your head.

Taming the critic or voice in your head

Being able to control the voice in your head or the critic that sits on your shoulder is paramount to your success as an actor.

You've done your preparation, you've made your decisions. Do you carry those decisions into the performance? Well, you can think that you will try to do them, but, as said, you must be moved and affected by what happens to you verbally and non-verbally in the scene.

So ask yourself, how do I let go as an actor in performance? How do I let go of the backstory stuff and the decisions that I have made once the performance starts?

Dealing with these three things will profoundly help you:

- Think of life – it is an improvisation. We don't know what's going to happen moment to moment. Unless we try to control people all day when we talk to them. So let go in the performance. See what happens. See where the scene goes.
- Ask yourself, do you control? How much do I try to control things in life? How much do I try to control during the scene? Surrender this need to control. Surrender this need to have the

scene go the way you want it planned. I suggest you try to stop yourself controlling in life as well as when acting.

- The critic. The critic in your head or on your shoulder has a desire to control and to often put you down. Learn to acknowledge and love your critic. In essence, you need to learn to tame it. Give it a name if that helps. Bob. Or Betty. Some people even call it Mum or Dad, but I suggest you call it a name that has no relevance to you.

It is good for you to know that the critic can also motivate you, guide you and encourage you to think and do things in certain ways – including to motivate you to learn your lines. So talk to the critic. Tame and train the critic by giving it guidelines.

A guideline such as: you need to stop it during a script reading or a performance. So, say to the critic in training: "During class or practice at home, if you speak up, I will tell you to be quiet. To go away and come back when I'm finished. I'll do this no matter how many times you speak up". You can even say this aloud to the critic.

Our minds are very powerful and can do many things at once. But when we act, we just want to listen and be in the moment. So, during a performance or audition of any sort, if the critic surfaces and speaks up and distracts you, say in your *mind*, "Go away critic. Come back at the end and I'll let you say whatever you want to say". Then continue the performance.

When finished, say, "Off you go, what do you have to say?" and listen to it. Let it have its say. It may say something useful. If it is just criticising stuff, you listen to it and then say, "Thanks". Then don't do what it says. All that really matters is that you have trained and tamed the critic during your performances.

I'll add this critical point: that from my experience and teaching, the actor who has gotten in touch with their *inner self*, through breath, chakra work and emotional work, will absolutely do better and have less negative talk going on in their mind while auditioning. Hence, here is yet another reason to work on the inner you.

The warrior in you

The warrior is an ancient word and brings up heroic connotations whenever mentioned.

I encourage you to bring out the warrior in you. I don't mean go out and fight or kill people or be overtly physically aggressive. I mean, work on bringing something out in you that has strength, focus, commitment and passion.

See yourself as a warrior and give yourself the licence to think it, feel it, be it. Having focus and strength to think and do and be anything is very powerful.

Try thinking you are the warrior, especially before you perform and especially before you have an audition or meet someone you want to impress, such as an agent or manager. You need to be strong when being an actor. Strong from within. The warrior will help you.

Rituals

I encourage you to create a list of rituals. A ritual list that you follow from the time that you get the audition, right up until doing the audition. Then after the audition, you should make notes on how well you think it went.

The rituals are a list of guidelines that you are to do for every audition. Noting that you have the time to do them before you go. For example, the breath vocal warm-up that I taught you (see pages 84 to 87), positive thinking and self-talk and hypnotherapy - as discussed below, the acting techniques as listed in this book, working with a friend, filling out the character background and script, play, scene charts as part of your backstory, etc.

Self-talk

Positive self-talk is advisable if you are nervous before an audition.

When you get a call for an audition, say this to yourself.

- I'm good enough and I'm going to do well
- I'll come from love not fear
- I'll de-sacredise (not worship or idolise) the occasion or the casting director of the project
- I'll do the best I can in the time frame permitted
- Whatever I do is okay

Then change the language as you are about to go into the audition or if negative self-talk eats at you:

- I'm good enough and I'll do well
- I've prepared the best I can in the time frame permitted

These statements are powerful and help you relax and alleviate anxiety. They are actually good for any occasion in life.

Self-hypnosis

It is best to do self-hypnotherapy when you are nervous before an audition.

Preliminary work: sit in a quiet place. Arms and legs uncrossed. Eyes closed. No music playing. No distractions.

The exercise: picture yourself going up into the sky. Go straight up out of your chair. Up past iconic things such as signs, churches, the beach, the clouds.

Then float along up in the air above the clouds and drop down into the audition. See yourself doing well at the audition. See yourself being given direction and you taking it well. See yourself concentrating and listening. All of this with your eyes still closed.

Then go back up into the sky and float along past this moment, into the future some more. Imagine going to a time fifteen minutes past the audition when you are in your car driving back home or walking somewhere and see *yourself happy* that you did a great job.

Then, still with your eyes closed, head *backwards* until you reach the audition. Retrace your steps, go back to parking the car, walking from the audition, saying goodbye, doing the audition and doing it well. Go back into the foyer where you were waiting, doing the sign-in, the walk back to your car, driving to the audition, your preparation at home etc. Go right back until you are back in your space at home in the present moment. Then open your eyes.

Checking exercise: Then you *test* yourself to see that you did it well.

Now, with your eyes closed again, go up into the sky again, and go along above the clouds and then straight down into the audition and see yourself doing well. Take note of how well you are doing and how relaxed you are. Then go straight back up out of the audition chair and back along above the clouds and then down into your body in the present day and open your eyes.

Upon reflection, if you looked relaxed in the audition room, and were doing well when doing the checking exercise, with no tension and no concerns, then you have done the exercise properly. If not, start all over again and go up even higher into the sky as you travel, and concentrate harder on the exercise all the way through it.

Keep doing the self-hypnosis exercise until you feel a state of relaxation and of *doing well* in the audition when you monitor it for the second time. That is, when you *tested* yourself to see how well you went.

From a metaphysical perspective, imagine that the self-hypnosis will be projecting a positive future for yourself. Because it will be.

The self-hypnosis exercises will absolutely help you do well in the auditions and you might find that you feel like you have been there, *at that audition*, before!

An aside: The AFL Richmond Football Club in Melbourne brought in a self-hypnosis expert. The players do many meditations, including projecting a positive outcome in the games they play. Over a four-year period, Richmond won three out of four AFL premierships and they finished third in the year that they missed out on the premiership. Wow!

The power of the casting director

Many actors have love/hate relationships with casting directors. They love the casting directors that bring them in for auditions, and they don't like the ones that don't bring them in for auditions. It's that simple.

Unfortunately, casting directors have so much power in the industry. Especially in Australia. Which is ironic as a lot of them in both the USA and Australia are people who started out wanting to be actors. At that stage, they had little or no power in the industry. They now have plenty of power.

Casting directors have plenty of power because, unless you are well known, before any producer or director can see your good work and cast you, the casting director has to choose you from your headshot and bring you into the audition or watch your self-tape.

An aside: Of course this is different if you are "packaged". Packaged is a very American thing and it means that the actors, writers, directors and producers are all often represented by the one major agency, such as William Morris/Endeavour, United Talent Agency or CAA. The agency creates the show, usually by doing a pilot, and then tries to sell it to a network television or a cable or streaming channel. If bought by the network or channel, all that particular agency's clients associated with the packaged show get work.

Casting directors soon *see* why some actors book work and why some don't book work. They also *see* real talent over people wanting to be professional actors but are never going to make it. This is because it is their job to see it.

What do casting directors see? Some of the things have been covered in this book. They see actors:

- relaxed and breathing well
- really listening
- who are focused
- with training
- creating characters with depth
- who the camera likes
- knowing how to work on camera or on stage
- taking risks and playing subtext
- emotionally connected and connected with the words they are saying
- they cannot stop watching
- who can be directed easily
- they like
- that seem to like themselves
- who are not needy or focused on simply getting the job

All casting directors like to discover these types of actors as listed above. Casting director Cameron Harris, who used to work at ABC television in Melbourne, discovered Rachel Griffiths. Cameron gave Rachel her first big break in television prior to her casting in the Australian feature film *Muriel's Wedding*.

Be nice to casting directors, but don't give them your power. It won't do you any good. If you do give them your power and sacredise someone, well then you have put them on a pedestal. This is not good for your psyche.

I have given away my power to casting directors and also to way too many other people in my life. In general, it never did me any good. I will never forget Roger Hodgman at Melbourne Theatre Company saying to me when I worked with him, "Don't put me on a pedestal. Don't sacredise me!" I profoundly thanked him for that.

You will do much better as an actor quietly thinking to yourself, "I will do very well today in this audition. I have prepared the best I can in the time frame permitted". Or if this works better for you, think this, don't say it, "No one is standing in the way of me playing this part. I am going to do a great job here today. No matter what!"

Be polite and humble in the casting session and then do a great job or the best that you can do that day. Then walk away. This strength, this sense of the warrior coming out in you, will serve you much more than giving away your power to the casting director. Respect them, but don't give them your energy and power.

Your main aim in an audition is to create an interesting character, serve the scene, and start a relationship with that casting director. If you are good, they'll remember you.

Sensitivity and handling pressure

I'll finish talking about auditioning by bringing up two very important topics: being sensitive and handling pressure.

How sensitive are you? I ask this as many artists are very sensitive. You have to have a tough skin and take a lot of rejections when working as an actor. You may not get the part because of your eye colour, your height, your ethnicity, your lack of chemistry between you and the other actor. Many, many different reasons, and you must accept you didn't get the part and move on.

If you think you are sensitive, work on the inner you and build the warrior in you so your self-esteem doesn't take a hard hit every time you don't get a job.

Also, ask yourself, how well do you handle pressure? I ask this as many actors put pressure on themselves when they want a big or important job. I know I did. For you, this could be a three-year contract on a soap opera, a lead in a feature film or a lead role on stage.

An actor must be able to handle the pressure of call back after call back, or working with TV network casting and producers for hours (if necessary) in mainstream television studios, or having fourteen producers sitting in the room watching your call back for, say, *Game of Thrones*. I experienced many producers in the room at call-backs when I auditioned in Los Angeles for television shows like *Malcolm in the Middle* and *Alias*.

You must learn to handle pressure. The best way to do this is to not pressure yourself. Play and enjoy after psyching yourself up with the warrior talk and then say, "Oh well, if I don't get it, I don't get it. I'll enjoy myself". Of course, this is easier said than done. So ask yourself, what will you do when you feel pressured? I suggest you practise a ritual grounded in relaxation and breathing and try to stick to it.

Learning Point Number Eleven

- Auditioning is an art form in itself. It requires the actor to empower themselves and to get to a point where they trust that what they have prepared will come out in the audition.
- The way you think and behave is very important.
- Develop your skills and always try to be professional.
- If you don't get the job, that is okay. Hopefully something else great will come up.
- Also consider self-hypnosis.

Chapter 7
Improvisation

Improvisation is all about using our imagination. Improvisation (or improv as it is called in the USA) is very important for the actor because it is, among many other things, the link between your script and your mind.

In this chapter, I explain how best to gain improvisation skills that will be invaluable in your acting career.

The importance of imagination

Imagination is an amazing thing. One of the reasons you probably became an actor in the first place is because, as a child, people kept complimenting you on your performances and your free, open expressive use of your imagination.

As children, by nature, we are very open to the use of our imagination. For example, maybe you were singing to your favourite band in front of the mirror holding a hair brush or the vacuum cleaner hose. Or you were dressed in a pretty frock and dancing around the house. Or you were imagining matchsticks were horses in a major sporting event, as you watched the match sticks race in the water down the roadside curb in the rain. Or you were building your own *Gilligan's Island* with mud in the backyard and pouring water around it like a moat. Or you were climbing on the roof of your house with your sisters' dolls and putting tomato sauce (ketchup), on the dolls and throwing them off the roof to emulate a horror movie or some other tragedy. All these scenarios mentioned are examples of the use of your imagination.

Please use your imagination. Work on trying to expand and keep an open mind when using your imagination.

Introducing improvisation

The more I teach, the more I realise that many actors lack imagination. They lack the ability to stay in the moment and imagine the location that they are in. They lack the ability to suspend disbelief one hundred percent about what is going on. They lack the ability to create interesting characters, locations and interpretations of what is going on with a script.

Without a script, improvisation is a form of expression that helps you play. Helps you create. Helps you imagine. Helps you work in with other actors. Helps you suspend belief and, indirectly, helps to prepare you for auditions. This is so because when a casting director or director gives you feedback at an audition, if you have improvisation skills, you are more likely to be able to adjust your performance and take the direction given.

Being able to improvise helps you tap into your imagination to help you produce creative work. It helps you create experiences that you have never experienced, or re-connect with experiences that you have had in the past. It often helps take you to places that you haven't been to. All this, in your own mind and body.

Whether you think you are funny or not, please do improvisation; you don't need to be funny. The longer I teach, the more I realise the importance of the use of one's imagination and improvisation skills.

Please see tips on how to help you with improvisation and how you can improve your imagination on pages 243 to 248.

Devise your own story

Firstly, allow yourself to be creative. Give yourself freedom to play. Feel free to create your own stories when you improvise. Being creative gives human beings such joy. Think of the 9 to 5 office workers. Many of them would love a job where they could be creative and improvise. You are lucky as an actor to tap into this. So go crazy, go nuts. Create whatever you want.

To improve your creative mind and to help you improve your improvisation skills, I suggest you watch cartoons. Cartoons will help you with being creative and help you to create characters and stories. Just think of the Road Runner, Donald Duck, Fog Horn Leg Horn, Porky Pig, Top Cat, Dick Tracy, Superman, Batman or the skunk, Pepé Le Pew.

Cartoon writers can write anything and then the animators can draw anything. They put no limitations on themselves or their own work because all they have to do is just draw it. They don't have to film it with human beings to make it into film and television. They just have to write and draw it. You can have this freedom in your work too. Play.

Learning the improvisation rules

There are rules in improvisation. Most importantly, accept what you partner offers you. Don't block them. Blocking is when someone says something to you, or asks you to do something and you say *no*, aloud, or you illustrate *no* with your body language, or you ignore what the other person is doing or saying.

This is taboo in improvising because it restricts creativity and causes the person who said this to think of something else to say or do.

So instead of saying no, try saying yes and see where it goes, or qualify. To qualify we say, "Well, I could do that, but why don't we do this first?" Or "I know I look like that, but I'm actually a [blah, blah, blah]". Or illustrate something else that you both could do first. Anything but saying the word no or turning away from the person and non-verbally saying no.

I recommended these suggestions because you do not wish to restrict your flow, your creativity, your development of the scene or the improvisation by blocking what you partner offers you.

Blocking is common practice for inexperienced actors. Usually because they are fearful. They feel it is easier to say no and to not be involved in the scene with their partner than to get involved. Of course, this totally stunts the scene's progression. And, of course, the actor is coming from fear, and this is the problem to begin with.

In addition, try not to ask too many questions when you improvise. I believe it is lazy for the actor to keep asking questions instead of making statements.

Statements are much better because you do not put all the emphasis and pressure on being creative, on the other person to answer you. Make statements and the two of you will move on together much more freely and create more fruitful scenarios. Then when you do ask some questions, later on in the scene, there won't be so much pressure on you both.

One final point to help you be better at improvisation (no secrets here) is to try to establish as soon as possible where you are, what you're doing and what is your relationship (for example, you are at the beach making a sand castle with your brother and sister or spouse). Preferably do this within the opening sentence or two.

With these things in place, both of you are in a better place to go forward on your creative journey, knowing where you are, what you are doing, and what your relationship is.

LID

I created these techniques, or ways of doing improvisation, when writing my curriculum in the USA in 2002. Practise them and you will do well in improvisation. The first one is an acronym:

L – stands for listen

I – stands for invent

D – stands for don't block

Basically, when you improvise, you should listen, invent stuff and don't block what is said to you.

The action

Physical action enhances improvisation because we, the audience, like to see people move and see people create things with their bodies. Give us action, some movement. Let yourself go. Create it with your bodies. We'll love it.

What will help the action is for you to follow this structure: **Create – Support – Add – Conclude.**

I created this concept many years ago doing Theatre Sports at both the St. Martins Theatre in South Yarra and the Victoria Arts Centre Concert Hall in the 1990s in Melbourne.

Theatre Sports is an improvised game where an Announcer/Compere will create scenarios and then teams of four actors will compete and be judged by a panel of judges in front of a live audience in, one-, two-, and four-minute, improvisations.

Simply, in a group of four actors: after being given the topic, we would all have input, whenever we wanted, but one actor from our group would be *responsible* for starting and leading the improvisation and he was called the *Creator*. Another actor was *responsible* for *Supporting* the story created. A third actor was *responsible* for *Adding* something new into the improv, and then the fourth actor was *responsible* for *Concluding* the improv. This worked successfully for us.

If you run with this concept while improvising, what you create as an individual or group should include:

- Beginning
- Middle
- End

And be:

- Created
- Supported
- Added to
- Concluded

These two ways of thinking when improvising will help you during the performance and help you have a complete story or skit or sketch.

The drama

As human beings we are attracted to drama. Even comedies have drama in them. In comedy, the drama is just presented or acted in a comical way, or by actors that we want to laugh at when we watch them act. All good improvisations have some kind of drama, even if it is silly drama, such as "I cannot get my shoe off", as in Samuel Beckett's play *Waiting for Godot*. Try to give your improv some drama, even if it appears silly.

The fun

Have fun. If you have fun, the audience will too.

The humour

Humour is subjective. You don't have to be funny to be good at improvisation. But it does help. Lighten up, and don't try to be funny —this will help you.

Why improvisation is important for the actor

Improvisation is excellent for the actor because it teaches you to allow components of freedom, exploration, creativity and spontaneity into your work.

As soon as a casting director, director, producer or teacher says to you, "I would like to give you direction and get you to do the piece like this...", you are much more open and likely to go where they want you to go, and do what they want you to do, if you feel you have the freedom and the confidence and the skills and the trust in yourself to be creative.

Creativity links in with imagination and freedom, and is all about having an open approach to your work.

One improvisation story goes like this: Robin Williams auditioned for the *Mork and Mindy* TV show many years ago by walking into the audition room and putting his body upside down against the wall with his head on the floor and started doing the scene from there. If this is true, how creative and risk-taking is that? And of course, Robin Williams booked the part, and the show launched his career.

Your imagination is one of the best tools that you have as an actor. How do you stand out from others? How can you make a great impact in your audition? How can your character be rich and have depth? Your ability to tap into your imagination sets you up to help you create these things. After all, it is your imagination, no one else's.

Actors that do stand-up comedy are often improvising and using their imagination as they go through their routines. This is so because many of them improvise with the audience while they are doing their routine. They do this by adding a reply to something that is yelled out, or they think of something else to say on the spot and add it in. Consider trying stand-up comedy as it will help open you up as an actor and give you a risk-taking element to your work. In support of this, stand-up comedy will be fun to do and will give you an avenue of freedom that you may need in your work. Robin Williams, Jim Carrey, Tom Hanks and many others, began their careers by doing stand-up comedy.

It is not a good substitute for the sort of formal training that is the main focus of this book. I say this because some actors choose to just improvise and not get formal training; and this is a worry because they often don't know how to breathe down into their bodies and use their breath and voice for support and effect. Also, their acting scene work often lacks technique, substance, connection, emotion, clarity and drama. In short, it lacks depth.

But do develop your improvisation skills because it will help you become a risk-taking actor. It will improve your imagination and, as a consequence, you will be able to adjust your performance on stage, on set or in an audition when given direction.

Have you heard the term, "magic moments"? In auditions, magic moments are often unscripted improvisation moments carried out by the actor.

They are improv moments where the actor shows a particular nuance of human behaviour, a natural reaction or utterance, in the moment.

Some ways to improve your improvisation skills outside of taking an improv class include:

- Start talking to strangers, about anything
- Talk to the person at the supermarket check-out
- Start telling jokes to people
- Write creative stories and then read them aloud. Then act them aloud with friends
- Form a group and improvise together
- Play out improv scenarios as buskers or on trains (non-aggressive ones, of course)
- Read
- Watch cartoons
- Daydream
- Play
- Do improvisation exercises with your friends or by yourself. Use your imagination and take yourself on a journey. Always have a location and yourself as the main character. For example, imagine yourself chasing a loose ball into a large concrete drain. Walk down the drain and have the circumstances change. Maybe it gets darker. Rats. Spiders. Water dripping on you. Gas. Pipe closing in on you. Hearing a noise ahead. Scream. Chains. It's dark. You follow the sounds. Discover the source of the sounds and decide what to do. And so on.

Learning Point Number Twelve

- Improve your use of your body, creativity, imagination, voice and auditions by doing improvisation.
- By practising improv, you are creating and expanding your creative skills as well as finding ways to help you stand out, especially in auditions.

Chapter 8
Making the right decisions: Student case studies

This chapter focuses on a number of case studies from my acting school classes. I have included them to help you make the right decisions in your acting journey. Some of the main points discussed in these case studies are *not* the way to think or behave.

Case study 1: Facing fear

Sometimes it is necessary to encourage an actor to overcome some issues.

Trying to impress the teacher is common behaviour from students. It is a kind of respect. When the developing actor is starting to improve their work and I am challenging them, some actors often try very hard to impress me. Trying hard to impress me, though, can often, indirectly, affect their confidence and ability to think clearly, while they are trying to do what I want them to do.

For example: I am working with a developing actor on camera and asking the student to pull their performance back for the close-up (not to be so big), and to act mainly through the eyes because I have them in a camera close-up. In addition, I am asking for more passion and commitment from the student in the scene.

While working recently with an actor in class on this topic, I had this problem. I could see that she wanted to do what I wanted her to do, but she was afraid she couldn't do it. She tried many times to back out of the exercise and kept saying, "I can't do this, I can't be more subtle and act through the eyes". I kept saying to her, "Yes you can and there is no such word as can't".

I called her emotional state for what it was and said to her, "You're nervous. You are nervous because everyone is watching you and the camera is on you. But if you just accept that, trust your technique training and go on regardless, you can and will do well". I worked with the actor five times on the same scene and eventually she did all the things that I wanted her to do.

I sat opposite her and looked deeply into her eyes. I had a look of encouragement and focused concentration. I read with her, like we were in a coffee shop drinking coffee as friends. I lowered my voice. I spoke softly and directly to her and soon she mirrored my physical actions and my tone and pitch and the volume of my voice.

An hour later, after resting for a while, she said smiling in front of the class, "I want another go. Can I go again". I was pleased. Her confidence and her ability to do the work had risen a level. A win for me as her teacher and a win for her in our partnership; on her journey to becoming a better actor and achieving her goals. Of course, in the process, she moved forward with developing her inner confidence through a positive experience.

In theory, what I did was encourage her. I supported her. I worked with her. I was firm but honest and as a consequence, I was influential and it worked. I didn't yell or raise my voice at her once. Good teachers, real teachers, generally don't need to. She faced her fear and she succeeded.

Case study 2: *You're so gorgeous*

There is no doubt that the more beautiful you are, the more the camera loves you. Yes, I know this is a generalisation, but please, I ask you to try to name multiple movie stars who are not attractive.

An aside: We can contradict this straight away by saying, to some people's eyes, Tommy Lee Jones is not a handsome man. I believe he is a movie star due to the following: his magnificent use of the tone of his voice, his use of pauses, his delivery of mundane text and his ability to perform for the camera frame. He doesn't overact, and he crosses the frame with his eyes as a part of his acting skills. This means he moves his eyes from one side of the camera to the other naturally. Much more on this in book two.

There are plenty of discussions that surround the topic that if you are attractive, your life is easier and people want to hang around and look at you. If you are "pretty" the camera will generally love you, and as a consequence some acting coaches may consistently flatter the ego of such an actor and not say too much else to them.

Generally speaking, this type of actor is often not challenged. They often don't take many risks because they have grown up with people constantly looking at them and telling them how *gorgeous* they are.

As an acting teacher, I have taught thousands of good-looking people. While working recently with an actor of this type in Hollywood, she mentioned that people tell her how gorgeous she is all the time. She confided in me. Telling me that people had always given her things, especially at school, where she didn't have to work too hard for good marks because of her beauty (and her cleavage).

This actor looked great on camera, but she had no idea how to personify risk-taking or subtext or how to create characters outside of playing herself or playing the *bitch*.

I asked her why she didn't do these things or know of these things, and yet, she just happened to have a four-year theatre degree from a USA University. She replied, "Teachers always said that as an actor, I looked so pretty, and not much else".

Well, what I did with her in class was to introduce her to as many concepts as I could. I introduced her to as many different ways of creating characters as I could. I had her doing neutral mask work and using her body in variable ways, to help her personify expression.

I had her crawling around on the floor creating lions, birds, giraffes and kangaroos. I did this to break her out of being still and not moving when acting. I went through all the verbal and non-verbal risks from my risk-taking chart and worked on them individually with her and then attached some to text for her to work with.

The list of risks that you can take are listed on pages 208 to 212. There will be a lot more talk about risk-taking in my second book, which focuses on screen acting.

I taught her the five acting techniques that I like to teach. I introduced her and profoundly encouraged her to explore text from Aristophanes to Shakespeare, Moliere, Beckett, and contemporary soap opera and film scripts.

After two years of training, this actor started to do three acting things very well. They were to:

- take risks
- have subtext in her work
- create characters

Of course, she still looked pretty. But now she is pretty and smart and trained and proactive in her career. She also now works a lot.

Case study 3: I want it all. I want it now

Some actors decide very early on that they want it all and they want it now. Some actors decide this once their confidence grows after booking some work.

As I mentioned in the introduction, Sir Laurence Olivier proclaimed, "Fellow students" at an Academy Awards presentation when he was in his eighties with a career that spanned more than sixty years.

We never stop learning and we learn in many different ways. I had one student in my school in the USA for a while who was in his forties. He was a writer, he was articulate, he spoke loud and had never really acted. When he joined my school, he was very passionate and keen to learn. He worked hard on trying to do things right and often would overact; even with his past history of *no actor training*.

Eventually I got him to where he was portraying some truth in his work and he started to book work. Well, then he changed. He would push me for more saying, "I want to work more, I want you to tell me more, I want it all and I want it now!" He actually used those words.

I tried to guide him, talking to him about how well he was doing, but also saying that he still had a lot to learn and it was a journey and I couldn't give him everything that I knew – *now* – and in one class. I explained how teaching people was a progression based on experiences and I mentioned the positive things about how well he was going on some of the new things I was teaching him, and I also mentioned some of the things that he didn't always do so well.

But this was not enough. First, he started rebelling vocally in a group class, and eventually he left the school branch in Los Angeles. He then chose to attack the teaching place that had given him his foundation, stating in a post-school assessment document that he "Didn't like the class structure and didn't like the school's cognitive approach to learning".

These comments, of course, were totally contradictory to his attendance and training and what he had said to me up until he left. He was generally always glowing about my teaching and the school that had taught him to be good enough to book work.

I am still proud of this actor and his achievements.

An important question to ask here is: what is meant "It all. I want it all"?

To answer that, I go back to one of the generally accepted principles of teaching and learning: that one idea follows another and that as the student gets better at understanding each idea, the teacher will introduce more complicated concepts, topics and activities. Think of Maths or English as an apt comparison.

Well, I explained to him how we learn, but he left the school anyway, *huffing and puffing and blowing the house down* in Little Red Riding Hood's Big Bad Wolf style.

Subsequently, this actor sent me work that he has done through *YouTube* and I can see the mistakes that he is still making. I see the overacting. I see he has still not learnt some of the things that I was trying to teach him to make him better, and so I know that he will not make it on a high level as an actor without more formal training.

I never allowed this actor into my master class. I felt his work wasn't strong enough. Perhaps that had something to do with it?

I know my heart is in the right place and I sleep well. I mentioned this case study to ask actors to trust your trained teacher. A teacher is there to guide you and make you better, in stages, when you're ready. As you get better, the work introduced to you will be more difficult. But please don't undermine or disrespect the teacher, or the way you have been taught that has helped bring you up to where you are now.

Instead, have faith and patience. Build and maintain trust with your teacher, and growth will come. Oh, and take the ego out of the equation. You can't have it all and certainly not all at once. And what is *it all*? Olivier didn't know, after sixty years in the industry.

An aside: In Japan, they have a visual art school where a student cannot progress into any other types of drawings, until they can draw a straight line and a circle perfectly, or to the level of acceptance from the teacher. Some students can take up to a year to do this. That's interesting, isn't it?

Which makes me think, after one or two or even three months of training to do karate, could I fight a karate world champion?

The writer/actor that I am talking about in this case study requested to link in with me on my LinkedIn a few years ago. I accepted his request. His profile reads, "Professional writer".

Above: A copy of one of the many thank you posters, books and cards that Paul received from students.

Below: The first AIDA New York poster playbill from 2005. Students performed off Broadway at the Abingdon Theatre, 312 W 36th Street, New York. The showcase was directed by AIDA New York staff.

Human Behaviour

Performed by A.I.D.A. Students

Director   Jemima Godsall

Assistant Director   Peter McClean

October 9th, 2005

American History X	Alex Pena, Justin Alba and Jerry Karan
Crimes of the Heart	Deirdre Woodburn and Margret Avery
Burn This	Barbara Allomand and Cory Shomake
Ghost	Eleanora Kartlin, Geraldine Smith, Jerry Karan and Nicole Kerushi
Extremities	Obi Lee and Cory Shomake
Monthy Python	Geraldine Smith and Karyn Pascoe
Heart in the Ground	Nicole Kerushi and Stuart Rios
Requiem for a Dream	Jerry Karan and Eleanora Kartlin
Closer	Naama Kates and Stuart Rios
Requiem for a Dream	Alisa Burkett and Jerry Karan
Hannah and Her Sisters	Laura Faith, Marta Witkowski and Naama Kates
Nip/Tuck	Karyn Pascoe and Justin Alba

Special Thanks to the Abingdon Theatre

Above: Newspaper story on Paul while living in Sydney in 2000.

Case study 4: Bad habits

Sometimes I find myself working on un-doing actors' bad habits.

An actor with bad habits often thinks they are better than they are. Some generally don't listen, they *act* listening. Some don't really use technique; they have gotten lazy. They don't breathe from the right place in their bodies. They don't take direction well; they think they make the right decisions with their first go. They are not too open to change. They think what they are doing is very good or good enough.

With this type of actor, I work on stripping this down and removing the *bad habits* of *bad acting* by always calling for and asking for the truth. Actors under my care usually start working with me by doing the Australian technique Dropping In The Text. Which includes the breath–thought–image–voice connection work.

This type of student is often reminded to listen, and where necessary, told to *stop acting*. This type of guidance is carried out while also giving positive reinforcement and nurturing them. In time, they usually adjust and grow.

In support of this, some questioning is always good. "Why are you doing that? Why did you make that choice? Are you stepping out of your work and sitting on your own shoulder watching yourself act?" I often ask questions like these.

As a teacher I like this sort of challenge. I like it because this type of actor is often in a state of paradox. On the one hand they have some ego because they have achieved some success and/or been around long enough to book work. On the other hand, they have been around long enough to develop those bad habits. They know they are doing some things wrong or not well enough to book more work. Or more credible, higher profile work.

I say to all actors, "Leave the ego at the door. Be open to exploration and change. Let's try some technique training and risk-taking work that has some foundation and substance to it".

With some actors I have said, "Once you have suppressed your ego somewhat, imagine you have never acted before.

Imagine as you pick up a new script and read it, that you are reading it for the first time. Imagine you know nothing. Imagine that when you are spoken to, you put yourself in a high state of alertness. You hear it, you decide whether what is said to you is good or bad and then you respond. In short, simplify what you are doing".

In time, I see the choices that the actor will commonly try to make. For example, *sleazy* man or *angry* man. I then say to the actor, "I see that all the time when you act. Try to give me something different. Perhaps give me some of this or some of that as you listen, interact and respond. And then let's build from there".

This work with the experienced actor, who has bad habits, is confronting and challenging; but I love it. Bring it on.

One final note on this, sad to say, but often true, just like most things in life, the older you are the harder it is to learn something new and learn to change. Actors with bad habits are often over thirty years of age.

Case study 5: Dealing with the demons in our mind

The following is part of a transcription of a conversation between a student and myself. Prior to the conversation, I wrote this on the whiteboard in class: *As an actor working on your skills, what is your biggest career challenge?*

> **Student writes:** I haven't had any role in anything except a couple of student projects and my biggest fear is going to auditions; because I'm a beginner and I feel that I'm not qualified enough. Maybe I'm hard on myself, but I always compare myself with others. My other challenge is English being my second language and having an accent.
>
> The other thing is most of the times I don't like myself on camera, for instance even out of many shots of my pictures

for a headshot, I don't really like any of them to present as *me*.

Paul writes in his notebook: that the actor wrote the following words:

Fear

Not qualified enough

Hard on myself

Always compare myself

It's a challenge as English is my second language

Don't like myself on camera

Paul introduces the topic "Love versus fear" then writes: What is perfection?

Student writes: I want to have and do everything in the best way possible. The right way that makes me and others happy.

Paul writes: What is the best way possible? What is the right way?

Student writes: The best way possible means I put all efforts to make sure things are right. But what is the right or wrong way? I guess it is what I think is right and I don't feel bad and I don't look bad in other people's eyes. But can we say is there any right or wrong?

Paul writes: What is right? What's looking bad in other people's eyes?

Student writes: That people think I'm a good person, this is probably part of the way I grew up. I want to feel good about myself and make others happy.

Paul writes: What is a good person?

Student writes: Someone who is likeable/loveable.

Paul writes: What is likeable?

Student writes: People like that person and enjoy seeing/being with them.

Paul writes: What is loveable?

Student writes: People always want to see them or be with them and they love that person.

Paul writes: Why don't you want to say anything else? Why the short answers?

Student writes: Because I'm thinking of many things, but it doesn't seem right to answer this question, because it brings the binary of: Good — Bad. Right — Wrong, etc. But it is in our mind all the time and that is what makes me or others judge things, which is probably not right.

Paul writes: What is bad?

Student writes: Compare to good. It depends on people's belief.

Paul writes: Who's judging?

Student writes: Everyone does!

Paul writes: What is right?

Student writes: Compared to wrong. These are hard words to use and to know exactly what they mean in any given situation.

Paul writes: Whose belief? Why do you care about people judging? What is wrong?

Student writes: People: including me, everyone around me, society, etc. Thinking of the meaning of the word *belief* according to the dictionary.

Acceptance of things without any given reason, makes it meaningless. Everyone has a different state of mind. That is the way I grew up in my culture, although I try to not care about people's judging, but I judge myself.

Paul writes: What has this written exercise drawn your attention to?

Student writes: We think about things unconsciously and that affects our behaviour. But if we deeply think about our state of mind, it is all nothing, nothing important that we can put our fingers on.

Everything is subjective, wrong and right, good or bad. These words can have different meaning for different people, but I keep using them, although by thinking about them when using it, it is meaningless.

Paul writes: Write ten things you can do to love yourself and not judge yourself while doing acting.

Student writes:

- Not thinking of what's right/wrong or good/bad
- Get rid of my belief system which might be based on nothing
- Be free of stress and fear
- Do not let the stupid thoughts come into my mind
- Don't compare myself with other people
- Don't think what others would think
- Enjoy the moment

- Let everything be
- Don't let the past experiences interfere with what is going on now
- Don't take things personally

Paul writes: ten answers to the following question and allow her to see my answers: Write ten things you can do to love yourself and not judge yourself while doing.

My answers are:

- Kiss my wife
- Teach the best I can
- Eat well
- Call my parents
- Read a book
- Walk and swing on the swings
- Eat Australian food and drink beer I like
- Visit friends
- Go to the gym
- Clean my skin
- Mend broken things
- Listen or watch live AFL football
- Listen to my favourite music
- Plan a trip
- Watch a movie I love

Student sees Paul's notes and then writes his own answers to the same question:

- Watch movies (which makes me happy more than anything else)
- Call my parents/email them
- Swim
- Skiing
- Dance
- Eat my country's foods

Chapter 8 | 167

- Eat nuts and seeds
- Drink fruit juice
- Play computer games
- Chat with sisters
- Going out with my boyfriend
- Telling jokes and laughing
- Taking care of myself
- Shopping :)
- Going to the beach
- Talk to my friends
- Driving around unknown places
- Singing along listening to music
- Taking more AIDA classes and learn as much as I can about everything (as long as there is no test)
- Drawing/writing
- There is only one person I have to answer to (myself)

Paul writes: Please think about what I spoke to you about – what have you learnt?

Student writes: I am too tough on myself. I must work on accepting me. Stop being fearful.

I then have a conversation with the student.

End of the transcription conversation between the student and myself.

I can see that this actor lacks self-esteem. I asked her to just try to love herself, and to not think about anything else that could hurt her, and to be herself. To be happy with being herself.

Acting is performing art and there is no such thing as perfection. Acting is an art. We should all love ourselves the way we are. In life not everybody is going to accept us, so don't bother trying to please everybody. So work on the inner you. It'll help clear your mind and make you stronger.

I also suggested to this actor to write these statements down and to say them aloud constantly:

- Come from love not fear
- Whatever I do is okay
- I'll prepare the best I can in the timeframe permitted
- I'm good enough and I can do well

These four simple and yet wonderful statements were given to me by Dr. Rod Farnbach, a psychiatrist who used to work with actors on performance anxiety in Melbourne.

These statements will help take the pressure off the actor. If applicable, I suggest the artist type, print and place these comments around their home and read them often. Place them in the kitchen, lounge, dining and bathrooms and around their work spaces, maybe even in their car, and work on loving themselves.

It is worth mentioning here that the above transcription happened in a time when there was limited awareness and acceptance of people with mental health issues, and no social media advertising encouraging the wider community to acknowledge and support them.

I have been dealing with actors' problems or concerns, if they agree to let me, for a long, long time. In support of this, the world today is so much better collectively on this topic. I am not saying that this actor had mental health issues. I'm simply saying that if their mental state is getting in the way of achieving success as an actor, if they agree to let me, the actors' skills will always profoundly improve with me working with them. I'm the conduit. The conduit between the actor and the booked work. I basically ask questions. I do breath connection work and let the student decide what comes up from them and what they need to heal or develop or let go in order to grow.

In closing, to state the obvious, in such scenarios, I generally remove the verbal discourse with the student. Instead, I get the student to write, and

I write too. This exercise helps open up students' minds to their fears and concerns.

Case study 6: Scared of the teacher

An actor performed a monologue for me in class recently. When asked how she felt she had done, she said, she was scared: "Scared of you".

When I was in college, I soon discovered that one of my educational aims was to please the teacher. To impress the English teachers with my intellect, creativity, interpretations and provocations. To impress my drama and acting teachers with my talent, my commitment to the work, the risks I would take, my ability to play subtext, create characters and implement technique. The more I pleased the teachers, the better marks I got.

I have always had the ability to teach, encourage and provoke actors into doing very good work. My staff, over many years, have often said to me: "You're not only a great teacher, you can see the students want to do good for you. You provoke and inspire them. You challenge them". My staff also often said, "Teach me how to do that, provoke and inspire them".

My point here is that there is a difference in the mindset between feeling challenged and feeling scared. One is a positive attitude, the other negative.

Running with the notion that every decision we make either comes from love or fear, choosing to feel challenged and wanting to impress the teacher is coming from love and positivity. It is not a bad thing.

Saying "I feel scared of the teacher" is coming from fear and not a good thing as it will often negatively affect your work. I encourage you all to think positively and to come from love. Because as a teacher, I do want to challenge you, and yes, I want to improve your work. But don't beat yourself up in your own mind during your training.

I'm glad this actor said what she did because we soon met one-on-one to discuss this in more detail and then moved forward with her training.

What we discovered through discussion was that this actor was recalling and relating her experiences back to adolescence, when her father spoke to her and asked her to do things. What she did was project her experiences onto me, how she felt when challenged by her father. This is not so uncommon behaviour for some actors.

It is also common that teachers have to identify and address this.

As mentioned earlier, our bodies have cells and they are made up of memory. So as this actor was in an acting situation where she was feeling something similar – most likely, a similar emotion to when she was interacting with her father – she recalled it. A similar feeling came up, in this instance, of being scared; scared of her father/scared of me.

So, what aided the fear? The fear of being judged is probably the answer. The fear of an astute watchful eye assessing her. Just like the experiences she had with her father.

Once we talked about this and the actor owned this in her mind and body, we moved on. The interesting thing is, this actor has subsequently booked some very, very awesome film roles, alongside well-known actors, and was generally already doing a terrific job. My support, understanding and compassion for her during this stage was both insightful and profound.

An aside: I talk in class sometimes about the Buddhist monks who had sinful thoughts and would go back to their room in the monastery at night and whip themselves with a strap for their sinful thoughts. I say to actors, don't beat yourself up, don't be the Buddhist monk; pat yourself on the back instead of whipping yourself or second guessing yourself or putting yourself down. Love yourself. Come from love, be challenged, not stressed.

Case study 7: Performance anxiety

An actor was performing a monologue in a technique class one day. This actor had just received bad news prior to leaving home and coming to class. In hindsight, perhaps he should not have performed.

His first performance with the new piece, undirected, was very low key. I gave him direction and he did the piece again. Again, it was very similar and low in performance value due to a lack of volume, lack of the use of the body, connection with the text, subtext and the lack of risk-taking in his work.

I began to try and find out what the matter was. I could see that when I spoke to him, he was listening, but not *really* listening.

An aside: I find *not really listening* way to common in the USA. Many actors I know have Attention Deficit Disorder or Hyper Attention Deficit Disorder. Perhaps it has something to do with the fact that Americans consume large quantities of soft drinks (sodas). Soft drinks contain excessive amounts of sugar, corn syrup, high fructose corn syrup and caffeine. All these things affect your concentration.

When I got up and demonstrated what I wanted this actor to do, this made him feel worse. I said, "I am actually doing this to help you. Not the opposite". I believe that by demonstrating, the actor can even copy some of what I am doing to help them get going.

Actors, if you see a teacher do this with you, please don't take it personally. It is done to help you. Go with it. I actually carry out *teacher in role* a fair bit in my teachings. I step into the work with the actors to help guide them.

An aside: this way of working is called "teacher in role", and it was taught to me during my teacher training days, where I was influenced by a drama teacher in England called Dorothy Heathcote.

In support of this action, there is an absolute similarity between me stepping into role with the actor in the space and directing them in different ways, as when a casting director works with actors in an audition, or when a director works with actors on set or on stage.

As an actor you have to be able to be adjusted, and if necessary, follow the lead of the person guiding you. If you cannot do it, you won't book work.

Having trust in yourself is very important here. Trust that you have the work in your mind and body and that you will connect with it when directed; because you can and you will. That's what the Australian Dropping In The Text layers are for. Learning to connect with the lines and trust yourself and the work.

Back to the actor's experience. The actor who had bad news prior to class was stagnant. I gave him some positive reinforcement and then asked him to perform again; he couldn't. He just stood there, in front of me and a class of about twenty-five actors and could not start again. I encouraged him. Students encouraged him and then he said, "I can't, I can't do it, I've lost it".

I asked him kindly once again and in the back of my mind I could empathise with him, as I had suffered performance anxiety way too much in my acting career. But he gave up and walked off the stage.

We talked later that night about his performance. We discussed his decision to stop and I asked him if he felt like, "A deer caught in the headlights?", and he said, "Yes. I felt stuck". We met one-on-one to discuss this in more detail and then, in time, we moved forward with his training.

What was happening, because his mood was low that night following the bad news he had received, was that when he was given direction and constructive criticism on his work, he chose to take it too personally.

I'm sure we've all done that right? His cell memory was probably actively recalling a past time when he was feeling low or had been criticised, and he could no longer concentrate and perform. His confidence was shot.

What would happen if this was a professional theatre show or he was on set or in an audition?

This is where acting is hard and not real at all. Acting is a bizarre vocation, isn't it? Actors have to let go of whatever is going on in their private lives, and live the life of the character, story, journey and the words of the acting job. Or at least, if applicable, try to incorporate their feelings into the work somehow.

Teachers have to be sponges and absorb all sorts of things from actors. But we do our best. This actor took some time off from acting and then came back to class with me. When he came back, I guided him through some classes to rebuild his confidence in his work and performances.

Performance anxiety can be crippling. I can remember auditioning for some very big contract roles on television, films and theatre that I really wanted. Performance anxiety profoundly affected my performances.

Many actors experience the same thing. Whether it be bad news that day or feeling sad because of a relationship break-up, or because they can't pay their rent, or because they want to prove to their parents that they can act professionally, or because they really, really want that part in that show – whatever the cause, many actors unfortunately suffer from performance anxiety.

One story from my life goes like this. (This scenario is from a few years before I won an on-camera award at the Ballarat Eisteddfod, adjudicated by Jan Russ.)

After five years of studying acting full time and with a degree in it, I went for an audition for a six-month contract on the television show *Neighbours*, in Melbourne.

I was so nervous, as I drove to the audition, I was listening to calming music by the Irish soloist Enya. I had waited years to get in front of the casting director Jan Russ, and I was finally there. Well, I couldn't relax, I couldn't concentrate and unfortunately, I couldn't trust my own acting ability and the choices I had made.

I did not do a good job and I did not get the part, and this feeling afterwards led me to do the following:

1. To see a doctor and then a psychiatrist who deals with performance anxiety

2. To consult an image consultant to help me with personal development on how I was being seen and interpreted by industry people

3. I employed a top-level acting coach who had worked at some of the best schools in Australia

4. I even bought my own camera and started having acting workshops with my peers

5. I started working on my inner self. This included reading some self-help books

All five things worked. All these things helped me grow and book acting work and, surprisingly, they are, in a way, a part of the foundations of my teachings and directing. And even the writing of this book.

If you suffer from performance anxiety, take action.

Get a teacher who knows how to work on it. Every actor has their own journey. Every actor learns slightly differently and every actor improves at their own rate. Excellent teachers are the conduit.

Case study 8: Ego is not a dirty word

So far, I have brought up the topic of the *ego* in performance and asked actors to surrender their ego to teachers to grow as performers. I would like to address this more here because ego can actually be a good thing for an actor too.

Without trying to sound contradictory, an actor needs an ego. They have entered a profession where they are being told that they are not getting the part, and sometimes *not even* being told at all that they are not getting the part. This is, of course, a common occurrence for most actors. Then when they are on set or on stage, an actor has to do what the director or producer tells them to do.

An actor's ego helps them continue on and to not give up acting after a short period of time or a few knock-backs.

Sometimes an actor has to draw on their own ego to help them achieve these goals. While working with actors, I have to deal with egos all the time. Once, while working with a male actor in a class, the actor could not strongly approach the woman in the scene and stand up to her and put her down. I asked the actor and even showed him what I would like him to do. As *teacher in role*, I guided him. This male was dumbstruck by the physical beauty of the other actor, so I introduced the ego.

I asked the actor to imagine this girl had broken off with him and he loved her. I added, "I want you to think that no woman breaks off with me! You always break off the relationship, but in this instance, she has broken it off".

The actor said, "Oh, you want me to be more assertive or aggressive as I say this or do this with my body?" I said, "Yes. Both the verbal and the non-verbal. Think about what it is like to be dumped". He said, "Women never break off with me". I said, "Great. Use that. Because this one just has".

Well, that was the trigger. This direction dramatically changed the scene and he did a great job, and, of course, he grew as an actor. A discussion followed, and afterwards this actor could clearly understand how to acknowledge and use the ego for the *good;* as an actor.

Like most things in life, find the balance. In this instance, find the balance between having an ego, knowing when it is present and knowing how to handle it.

Our egos have roots in our values, mores and ways of socialisation. The smart actor can identify it. For example, a male actor might think, "Ah, yeah, my dad was angry a lot and defensive and I inherited it from him", or we might find, consciously or subconsciously that we do our best work, at auditions or on set when we feel cocky or confident in ourselves.

Again, take note when it appears and when it needs to be controlled and when you need to pull it back a bit. Because nobody likes *a know it all* or an aggressive or arrogant person. When dealing with the ego, humility is always a good thing to remember.

A footnote for males: it is harder for you to recognise and control the ego than it is for females.

Case study 9: You want the truth – you can't handle the truth

Tom Cruise sprouts the line "You want the truth – you can't handle the truth!" in Rob Reiner's feature film *A Few Good Men*. We all think we want the truth, but sometimes actors really do not want to hear it.

I'm Australian. Candidness is our middle name. We'll say it how it is. But we are generally not rude or cruel.

From my teaching experiences, if it is not positive feedback, some American actors, much more so than their Australian counterparts, do not want to hear the truth, no matter what they say. I say this based on my experiences, and also with an awareness that there is so much bullshit spoken in the US entertainment business.

This is especially true in Los Angeles where I have experienced actors who, half the time, don't know *what is the truth and what isn't*. They are confused. They don't know who to believe.

Once I had three actors go through the same *teacher giving feedback* experience. I'll preface this by saying that what I say comes from the heart and is the truth as I see it.

When I spoke to all three actors I did it kindly, with a soft voice and delivered my comments with a teacher's love – a love wanting to see growth. In other words, a teacher's support and provocation.

It just so happened, in this case study, the first two actors were from the USA, and when I told them what I wanted them to work on, what they were doing wrong on camera, I could see they were severely affected by what I said.

I am really good at reading body language and so of course I addressed the topic again after class. I did the *same thing* with all three actors.

After the discussion, the two Americans were feeling low and weakened; they left that night and never came back. Which is not a common occurrence, by the way.

The third actor, an Australian girl, also feeling low and weakened, firstly, shook my hand, then hugged me, verbally thanked me and walked away saying that she now knew she had lots to work on and appreciated my honesty, observations and candour.

She went on to study with the school for about a year and a half.

I drew this comparison between two American actors and an Australian actor because I think it is relevant. As a teacher, I do not stand actors in class and strip them down (like many American teachers do), and secondly, actors hear constructive criticism from teachers and people in the industry a lot.

Perhaps American actors are confused and perhaps they are used to hearing so much bullshit all the time that they do not know what to believe? Maybe then, some American teachers just say whatever the actors want to hear?

Was my constructive criticism put to the two Americans too delicately and analytically, in a way they were not used to? So, they went away really hurt and perhaps gave up acting? I can only surmise.

Most importantly here, I have found that an actor's mindset and behaviour usually have some correlation with them thinking the following things: that they are ready for representation, ready for work, ready to perform, perhaps in a showcase to industry, and/or to be referred for some professional acting work.

But sometimes they are not ready. Some actors absolutely have stars in their eyes and blinkers on, like horses. They do not hear real constructive criticism and often blame the teacher for their lack of success. Actors please be open to hear constructive criticism.

An aside: I think it is interesting how these two American actors left my class and never returned. In case you are wondering, most of my actors over the nine years and one month of my school in Los Angeles, between 2002 and 2011, were from the USA. (My school is operative again nowadays, by the way.)

But maybe there is something to think about with the two American actors often being in classes where they are yelled at. Maybe they were not used to *my* calming tone and detailed analysis?

Also, did they feel pressured to succeed at their vocations in a society in which if you don't succeed, you could end up homeless? More on this topic in my next book where I compare Australian and American actors and acting training.

Here is another example of not being able to handle the truth. One actor I trained in Los Angeles for a few years was a relatively poor actor.

Aged in his thirties, he had a full-time job, and was not a quick learner. It took me years to get him up to be anywhere near performance standard.

Even when he performed, I felt he still wasn't good enough and I copped a lot of flak for putting him in an Acting Showcase that was open for the public and the industry to see. But I did it because I cared about him and wanted him to have an opportunity for the entertainment industry to see him. He had also asked me many times if he could go into this showcase.

After the showcase, which was on stage, in which he did grow (I was quite pleased), he wanted to make a show reel on tape of some of his work so he could upload it online to help him get more auditions. I suggested he *wait* a couple of more months as he had just gotten off stage and, in the previous weeks, he had just gone back to working in front of the camera.

And he was struggling in the camera class. Stage acting and screen acting are very different. Unfortunately, all this actor heard was *you don't think*

I'm ready. He actually said those words to me and then he left the school immediately. Over my thirty-two years of teaching, as of 2021, I've noticed that a few students didn't just leave; they take passing shots at the school as they go.

The expression *you can lead a horse to water but you can't make it drink* seems apt here. I'm a teacher. I'm not *a* genie in a bottle giving out natural talent and skills. Or intellect. Or imagination.

We teachers simply must absorb this type of behaviour from actors – which sometimes, but not often, is a verbal attack. We must learn from it and move on and do what we do best: teach people to get better.

This actor wanted the truth. I know him well, he studied with me for a couple of years. I candidly gave him the truth and he couldn't handle the truth, and I was rewarded by him leaving the school. Oh, his work on tape was just okay. Not good, not great, just okay. Did he get any work from it? Not that I am aware of.

While I was writing this book, this actor, as well as some others who had left in a huff, returned to being trained by me over a two-year period. He has matured a lot. Unfortunately, though, he is not booking major work as an actor yet. But he does have seventeen IMDB credits as of June, 2022. Some actors just won't wait until they are ready, will they?

Learning Point Number Thirteen

- Can you relate to some of these case studies? Can you empathise with the actors? Can you have an understanding of where the teacher is coming from?
- I have included these case studies here to help you make the right decisions.
- A common thread in these case studies is: if you value the teacher's opinion, then hear it and take it on board, don't take it personally.
- Have patience and work with your teacher, not at loggerheads with your teacher.

Chapter 9
Training the experienced actor

I'm generalising here, as I am sure there are exceptions, but most actors have had to work hard to get where they are in their careers; and they work hard to stay there.

In the previous chapter, I spoke a bit about the experienced actor under Case study 4: Bad Habits (pages 162 and 163), I would like to talk a little more about this topic here.

Keeping up skills

Experienced actors who regularly book work like to be in class because they like to keep up their skills, keep their mind ticking over with text and their creativity flowing.

When working with an experienced actor I like to give the actor room to move. What this means is, sometimes just staying out of their way and letting them do the work without too much comment or guidance. This is often a good thing to do, especially when beginning to work with them.

Let them act. Give them room to play and, where applicable, advise them along the way. I try to not *top them* or think I need to impress them because, for the most part, this is unnecessary.

When working with an experienced actor, I talk to the actor about what their philosophy on acting is. I say to them, "What are you doing that helps you book work?" I then move onto saying things like, "What can I teach you? What do *you* think you need help with? What concerns do *you* have at auditions? What is going on in your mind?"

All of these questions might seem general, but they are not. The experienced booking actor knows what works for them. They know how to book work. As with most things in life, open, honest communication is the way to go; and then we take it from there. When having discussions with the experienced actor, a new topic to explore usually emerges for us both.

Discussion is usually followed by practice. For example, because of the nature of the entertainment business, experienced actors often get cast in similar roles all the time.

Even many celebrity actors find it hard to branch out into different roles or different genres in which to act. Believe it or not, the ability of Robert De Niro, Jim Carrey and Robin Williams to successfully move between comedic and dramatic roles in films is not the norm.

The experienced booking actor is also often in a state of paradox. On the one hand, this type of actor has an established ego attached to their work; and on the other hand, they know they are doing some things wrong or not well enough to book, let's say, more rewarding work.

More rewarding as in, say, working at a higher level to what they usually do. For example, moving from a co-star to a guest star credit on a US television show is often not easy and takes time and work.

As their teacher I focus on where I think I can help. This could include affirming and reaffirming what the experienced actor *already* does well. Sometimes it is simply trying new techniques or just having them hear another voice. A different voice talking to them to help them grow.

Taking away the bag of tricks

When the experienced actor works with me, I also say to them, "Please show me your bag of tricks. Show me what you do well". This is then added into the mix. One activity that experienced actors like is when I get them to list their bag of tricks. The tricks they use to book work. By following what they *do* do, it is then fun and a challenge to introduce them to an experience where I take them out of their comfort zone by saying, "I don't want to see your habits, I don't want to see your bag of tricks. What can we do that is new in your work?"

I love working with experienced actors as they challenge themselves and want to improve and learn new techniques. Or else, work at improving their comedic and dramatic abilities.

As said, Robert De Niro is a perfect example of an actor who did a lot of dramatic work and then, more recently, has worked in comedic roles in films. Whether you like his comedic work or not, *good on him* as an actor for working on developing his comic side of his *acting chops*.

Of course, the experienced actor may want help with emotional connection with text, or to learn how to cry on cue, or work out bad habits that they have developed, etc. I love working with the experienced actor on these things. By watching their stage, film and television work, we can also pinpoint some issues or problems and then move forward to solve them.

I do this through exercises and performances. For example, I ask them to start a scene in a neutral state. I ask them to have made no decisions whatsoever and to just hear the first line and explore anew from there. Sounds easy, but for some actors it is a challenge. Experienced actors generally love working on this exercise.

For example, beginning neutral, where you do not immediately display how you're feeling or what your *subtext/want* is, takes concentration, effort and trust. You need to be palpable. You are rooted in neutrality and about to go on a journey of performing without your *bag of tricks*.

Australian actor Sam Worthington often begins scenes in this position. When we look at him at the start of a scene, he looks grounded and neutral. As he explores, we want to watch him. We want to see what he discovers. No wonder Sam became a leading male actor, because as he explores and discovers with his whole mind and body and voice, we explore and discover with him.

This is actually quite profound as audiences need to be introduced to new things going on. As an audience, we really like exploring and discovering along *with* the character.

One of the main objectives of the series regular in television or the lead role actor in films and on stage, is to take the audience on the journey. As the actor discovers new things, new people, new drama, changes of plan or direction, they are taking us, the viewers, along with them.

To help understand this, think of all plays, all films and all television as a journey; an adventure that we are going to go on. As an audience, we subconsciously are conditioned to acknowledge and adhere to this formula as we watch. Well now, think of it consciously, as it is the leading actor's role to be that person for the viewer. To draw attention to what is going on and move the story forward.

By putting the experienced actor into this state, they are likely to create new work because they are exploring new territory. Then the teacher and student can discuss what the actor learnt. What were their new discoveries? For example, "What was it like when you couldn't smile like you usually do?" or "What was it like when you couldn't be angry in the scene like you usually are?" Then move on from there.

Of course, talking in one-on-one sessions, viewing and analysing their work and introducing them to new acting techniques, are all new things that the teacher can do with the experienced actor as well.

Learning Point Number Fourteen

- Even experienced actors need to learn and grow and keep practising.
- Stripping the actor of their "bag of tricks" is a good way to start to explore new things and help improve their work.

Above: Teaching in Japan: Tomofumi Akie san is listening to Paul carefully in his role as translator at the Stone Wings Acting School in Tokyo.

Part 2
Practice

Chapter 10
Having the right attitude

Before I get to the nitty-gritty of acting practice in the next chapter, I would like to talk about something that is just as important as having the right practical skills: having the right mental attitude.

A general psyche to play and win

Anyone can win. Any actor from anywhere in the world.

Australians are generally a curious people and, like Americans, we do open ourselves up to the world. Especially in relation to the entertainment industry and learning about different acting techniques. I am sure this has something to do with Australian actors and even directors and people who work as crew, are doing so well worldwide.

The USA has a very large population and entertainment industry infrastructure. This infrastructure is much more accessible, and profoundly financially supported, and hence is much more available than, say, the Australian entertainment industry, which focuses on sport through both its federal and state governments.

American actors also put themselves in a position to play, learn and win. Part of the reason is because of their general openness to receive people from throughout the world. *In theory*, they are in a position to receive information and education from foreigners, including me, and my teachings.

Some psychologists say that it is much easier to choose to be negative than positive in life. The struggle for many people is to keep choosing to be positive; or at least to be neutral. If a person is not achieving their goals, their dreams in life, this can cause friction within the mind, leading perhaps to depression and much worse.

This is one of the reasons why a teacher/coach, or mentor, is vital for the growth of a student. This is because the teacher, where necessary, supports, educates and encourages the student's growth; sometimes helping them grow out of depression and frustration.

This is done through listening, creativity, reinforcement, the teaching of skills and celebrating minor successes.

One of the reasons I encourage actors to get *representation* is to give themselves some minor success. This can be in the form of a good audition, a good meeting with a casting director, even a role in a student play or film.

All we have to remember is that everybody cannot win. Everybody cannot be a movie star. Unfortunately, everybody cannot achieve all of their goals. But I suggest you can all try.

Achieving your goals

To help you achieve your goals as an actor, I suggest you adhere to these precepts:

- Treat everything that you do for your career, training, work, marketing and networking with total professionalism
- Turn up on time: on set, on stage, in class
- Consistently turn up to class or auditions. One of my acting teachers in college, the wonderful Yoni Prior, said to me, "If you're not in class, you're dead".
- If you like the teacher and the school, trust that they are doing the best thing for you. I say this because some actors think they know better about their own work than the person who is training them. This makes me think, *why are they in class?* I have been personally blamed by an actor for him not booking work or doing good work in class; I've heard this from other teachers too. Trust your teacher, as opposed to arguing and defending yourself all the time
- Don't procrastinate or self-sabotage in any way

- Be diligent about homework
- Read, read, read!
- Try to do what you learn in class as an actor – in life. For example, train yourself to look sideways as opposed to up and down to help your *on-camera* skills. When talking to people, try to guess what their *want* is, their subtext. Try to stay focused and really listen to what they are saying
- Observe other people's body language. If you see an interesting character, think what is he doing verbally and non-verbally that makes him interesting? After all, acting is imitating life, isn't it?
- Watch actors work. Watch actors you like and try to analyse what they are doing.
- Steal from other actors and try to emulate the things that they do
- Become a risk-taker. Actors who take verbal and non-verbal risks get call-backs, book work and do better work than actors who do not
- Try to put yourself in the position where you don't know what you're going to do next. If you are truly in the moment and listening, you are open to anything and everything
- If you build up a relationship with an acting coach or teacher, stick with them, because actors who cruise the schools often end up not knowing what technique to use. I see this happen consistently in Los Angeles, where actors think the correct thing to do is to cruise the schools and take a little bit from here and a little bit from there. Which, of course, is okay if that works for you and you book paying work
- Get a camera. Cameras are cheap nowadays. If you want to work in film, television or commercials, buying a camera and working with your peers on scripts could be one of the best investments you could make. Seeing what you are doing on-camera when you act will help your training and acting work overall.
- Don't try to nail it. As mentioned in Chapter 6, as an actor, you want to explore and not try to nail a scene or a script. Because if you do, there is an element of sitting on your own shoulder and

watching your work as you try to nail it. It is performing art, so explore, play, try to achieve your subtext, but don't worry if you don't. It is the thought of going on a journey and the exploration that will help make you watchable and help you take risks.

Finding different ways to be watchable

Every actor wants to be watchable. Being watchable will profoundly help your career. But what is "being watchable?" Are you watchable? As previously mentioned, I believe acting schools choose actors they want to train based on seeing actors they want to watch. I used to do the same sometimes in my school in the USA.

The school's thought process goes something like this: if I, as a coach or teacher – who has seen many actors perform over many years – want to watch you act, then the general public most likely will too. Sounds simple, right?

Some actors we just want to watch. Some are born with the gift. Surprisingly to note, many of the actors who are born with it are lazy. Another generalisation I know, but true.

Can we watch you too? Even if you are not one of those *lucky* actors, well, with work, a good teacher can improve your *watchability*.

Being watchable means that we want to watch you. We are interested in what you have to say and are moved by your character's journey and what you are doing and feeling.

While watching you, we often also have our animalistic attraction and senses buttons pushed too. Such as, physical attraction and, ridiculous as it may sound, often a desire to want to hang out with you or even have sex with you.

To help you be watchable, I suggest you work in the following areas. These are not in any specific order. They are all important. Some of them may not seem that applicable, but they *are* applicable, because a naturally relaxed mind, body and soul will permeate a strong grounded message.

- Breath. All acting begins with where we breathe from and to in our bodies
- Technique. It is the foundation of your craft
- Listening. If you don't listen really well, you won't make it
- Posture. Stand tall and confidently
- Confidence. Fake it, if you have to, until you make it
- Education. Be smart. I don't know a dumb actor who has made it
- Training. Always have it and give yourself licence to grow
- Versatility. Learn about, and act in, all genres and with all literature from the Ancient Greeks to contemporary times
- Vulnerability. Show it. If we are not moved by your character's situation, why should we watch you?
- Diet. Eat and drink well. Educate yourself on how certain foods and drinks are good for you and others not good for you. *Chinese, Japanese and Korean* people do this very well
- Belief. Work on it all the time. Educate yourself on it and develop trust
- Positivity. Surround yourself, your meditations and your life with positive people
- Imagination. The only limits to our imagination are the limits we put on ourselves. Use your imagination as an actor in theory, rehearsal and performance

Learning Point Number Fifteen

- What is your general psyche to win?
- Consider writing a list of positive items that you can do and work on to help your career.
- Consider applying my different ways to be watchable to help you

Above: Paul conducting "housekeeping" with the AIDA students in 2007 in Hollywood. At housekeeping, the students talk about their small and big successes, such as: booked work, call-backs, meetings with industry people, networking, headshots, the growth or thoughts that they are having as an actor, and so on.

Chapter 11
Acting on stage

Acting on stage is about learning how to tap into the energy of yourself, your fellow actors, the audience and the room or theatre. All of the things mentioned in this section will help you improve your stage acting, particularly your presence – presence on stage or in a space and/or at an audition.

How to enter

Entering onto a stage is an art. Experienced actors almost look like they are acknowledging the audience, without speaking, when they enter. Especially when they first enter.

It is simply a look towards the audience as they enter, straight out in their direction, in fact. If done well, it is very powerful. The look is quick; it usually pans from one side of the room or theatre to the other and it is done with confidence, authority and subtlety.

It works. Try it. Don't wave at an audience member or acknowledge the audience openly in any way as this will immediately defeat the strength of what you are doing.

Stage etiquette can be tricky, but always try to remember that the audience can see you better and hear you better if you are turned out and even looking straight out towards them.

These subtle skills are good for all acting, including performing on camera and at auditions for on-camera work, where you need to read with other actors. This is because you are turning out towards the audience (in this case the camera), and making it easier for the people watching your work to see you.

Presence

Some people just naturally have a knack for standing there and speaking and we want to look at them and/or listen to them.

What is presence? How does one acquire presence? This question always makes me think of the open auditions at an acting school in Sydney. At this school, when actors auditioned, the teachers used to say in the 1980s and 1990s, "We don't know what we're looking for this year; but we'll let you know if we see it". I, or no one I know, ever heard a staff member from this school, at the open auditions, say the words, "We've found it. We know what we're looking for this year!"

I've been told by a staff member at this school that when holding open auditions, the staff said the same thing every year. Of course, what they were looking for was *je ne sais quoi*. Meaning, the actor that they are watching, has something. We don't know what it is but it is profoundly watchable.

Je ne sais quoi actors with stage presence take the space as they speak. We, the audience, want to watch and listen to them and we don't know why.

Being able to stand there and speak, where we, the audience, want to look and/or listen to you, is called one aspect of stage presence. An important one.

Cate Blanchett apparently *blew them away* at her acting school audition, fellow actor Rachel Griffiths is quoted as saying. Apparently, Rachel was there auditioning at the same time and everyone loved Cate.

What if we don't have the stage presence of a Cate Blanchett? What if we don't have stage presence at all?

I can teach anyone to act. I've proven it time and time again. I say to my actors in training, "Do you want me to listen to you? Why am I going to listen to you?" The answer I give them is because I tell them that what you are about to say and do is really important to you. You must be heard. You will demand an audiences focus because it means so much to the character you created.

But don't say this aloud, I say to actors, you just think it. Raise the stakes for your character and for what you are about to say, and we are more likely to want to watch you and listen to you.

This is what I mean when I talk about acting on stage (or screen). I tell actors to tap into the energy of themselves.

In support of this, the other way to improve your watchability is to always think I will play everything for real. I will suspend disbelief. Whatever is happening, whatever is going on and is affecting my character, I'll believe in it one hundred percent.

How to move on stage

To help actors tap into the energy of other actors, the audience and the room, it's important to know how to move well.

The basic principle is you should try to face the front of the stage, called downstage, as much as possible. Unless, that is, you are directed not to do so for specific reasons. These reasons most likely would have something to do with the play and/or what is going on.

Open up your feet

When standing, always try to make sure your body language is open and turn your feet slightly out, so you open up the body. If you open up or turn your feet outwards so they are on slight angles, you will be opening up your body even more.

This way the audience can see you better. Most importantly, audiences will see your face. This will also help ensure that your voice is being heard because the sound of it is going in the direction of the audience.

Position your feet like in the diagram below. Open up the hips and nonchalantly look out towards the audience. Dancers would call this "almost 2nd position". Imagine you are almost about to do a ballet plié.

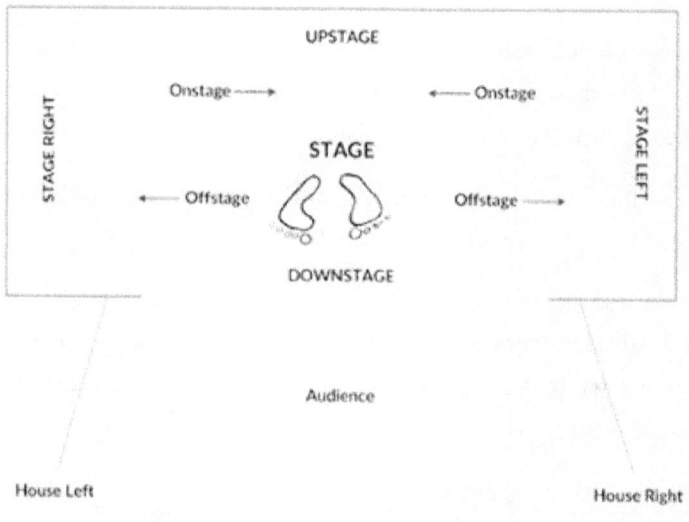

Turning

When you turn, left or right, turn downstage. Turn the front of your body towards the audience and not your back. This way we will see your turn. Turn the feet out, like the diagram above, and this will help you move around freely and keep your body language open.

If you are moving *stage left* (your left is as you stand on the stage facing the front), move the left foot first and commence walking. If you are moving *stage right* (your right is as standing on the stage facing the front), move the right foot first and start walking.

Where to look

Look out towards the audience as much as possible without losing connection with the people you are talking to on stage. Move your eyes and focus between the two. But always remember, on stage you can look just a little bit at the other person and or gesture in the other person's direction and keep talking. Especially if there are only two people on stage and/or you say their character's name.

You can even not look at them for a while, and we will know that you are still talking to them. This is because an audience suspends disbelief and is looking at the whole stage at once. Australian actress Robyn Nevin is one very experienced stage actor I worked with at the Melbourne Theatre Company who does this so very well.

Robyn will constantly look out at the audience and often simply gesture towards the other actors after she has made initial eye contact with them in a conversation. Robyn is performing for and with the theatre and its audience.

One final note on this, when I say look out towards the audience, I do not mean that you gesture, acknowledge or address the audience in any way (unless doing Brecht's epic theatre), or you have been directed to do so by the director or the writer of the work. Just look out in the audience's direction.

Where not to look

Try not to look too much at the floor or the ceiling or in the wings of a theatre. The wings are the two sides of the stage.

Looking at the floor or the ceiling has been such a concern for me for teaching many actors that I have trained in the USA. Many acted to the floor or to the ceiling in class and wanted to do the same in industry showcase performances that I directed too.

I think that some actors do this because of habit and perhaps because of a fear to really connect with the other person, or commit to openly expressing themselves.

I also feel that this can be a cultural habit as well. And it is catchy. So, beware. It is such a problem sometimes that, in the USA, I had to place letters up on the back wall of the theatre that we worked at in Hollywood saying: LOOK UP HERE. Seems silly, but it worked.

Upstaging

Upstaging is when you are looking upstage, towards the back of the stage or the audition room, and the other actor is looking downstage towards the audience.

If you are looking upstage as you look at the other actor, we see the back of your head or just your profile. Your voice is going upstage into the back wall or into the back of the stage in the theatre. If this happens to you, you may have been upstaged by the other actor. We, the audience, see all of the other actor's face and head clearly. We also hear them better because their voices are coming out towards us, in the front. But we don't see or hear you clearly at all. Upstaging is taboo in theatre.

Distance between you and the other actor

The closer you are together on stage with another actor, the more you need to turn your feet out towards the audience and keep your body aligned with the other actor. If you don't do this, upstaging may occur.

If you are standing slightly upstage (towards the back wall), and the other actor is having to turn upstage to talk to you or address you, they are turning their body away from the front (downstage), towards the audience, and you are consequently upstaging them.

You look great. Everyone can see you clearly. But the other actor is closing themselves off from the audience and their voice is most likely going upstage as well towards the back of the stage. So, don't do it.

If close to other actor/s, I suggest you stay on their line – parallel to them. Unless directed not to do so.

Also remember, education is power, so if you see someone upstage you, you can align yourself or slightly subtly move them to help make you both look good. To subtly move them into alignment, gently touch their back and move them towards you or step back towards them so you are alongside them.

Interestingly enough, the further away you are from your fellow actor, the more you can change the dynamic of positioning and create angles and still talk to them and turn out to the audience, and stay in these positions for some time: à la Robyn Nevin again.

General rule: if close to the other actor, align your body with theirs. If far apart from them, it doesn't matter so much. The angles generally look good.

I hope this helps you understand why and how to stand and how to *not* be upstaged as it is important for an actor and also important for camera auditions too. Because if you are upstaged, the camera won't see or hear your work clearly either. So, remember, upstaging others can also happen when reading or acting in front of a camera.

Learning Point Number Sixteen

- Knowing how to move well and correctly on stage so you are seen and heard and not upstaging anyone is an art.
- Learn how to do it. This helps you have presence on stage.

Chapter 12
Australian techniques: Dropping In The Text

In Chapter 4, I explained how to do the layers as you drop the text into your body. It's a good idea to revise that explanation before doing the exercises in this chapter.

To begin the layering system work of Dropping In The Text, I suggest you do the work with this monologue below. This Dropping In The Text work works well with both the chakra alignment work and the emotional exercises as mentioned on pages 88 to 93.

The script chosen for the layering process is a female monologue called "Knowing". I cannot find the writer of this chosen monologue. So please excuse me for stating the writer is unknown.

As you can see in the next paragraph, with this monologue "Knowing", to make it easier for you, I have already broken the first paragraph of the script down into beats and put an action word from the Actions handout on page 000 on the first three beats. Feel free to alter the beats and chosen actions if you wish. In this monologue below, the beat symbol / is in bold and action words are underlined.

KNOWING

To introduce /   to explain

Here's what I know / I know that you were my hero /

/ to compare

and the first best friend I ever had who was a boy / and that you taught me all the lines to Slapshot, / and how to kick anyone's ass at video games, / and how to drink Tequila like a man, / and how to be brave. /

But it's hard to be brave when there's so much I no longer know. It would be so much easier if I just knew that you were gone forever – even to learn that it had been horrible or painful or terrifying at the end. To find out, once and for all, if you did go into that river. If the raging waters you loved so much took you from me – even to know that you went willingly. Or to discover if any of the hundreds of tips and theories were true. Did you get car jacked or kidnapped or worse? Or did you just decide to disappear – to walk out of the bar that night and leave your life behind. Was it all just too much? Too hard?

Because if that's the case, then you weren't ever as brave as I thought you were – if you're hiding on some Mexican beach somewhere – drinking Tequila just like you taught me, then frankly, you're a coward. And the most despicable selfish bastard I've ever known.

And I should hate you forever, and never speak to you again – but the other thing I know is that I would forgive you in an instant if I could just see you again. Just for a minute – in a busy airport maybe, or in a city where I've never been, or in any of the millions of crowds I've scanned for your face. I would at once hate you and forgive you and finally, thankfully, know.

Please break the rest of the script down into beats yourself and put an action word from the Actions list on page 206 on each beat.

Please follow the step-by-step instructions on what to do next in Chapter 4. A tip – don't rush, take your time.

On the next pages are a list of **Actions** and **Wants** that my school uses. The actions are all verbs.

Above: Actors enjoying a class with their teacher.
Below: Actors feeling in-tune with their bodies as they work on their concentration skills.

AIDA
INTERNATIONAL

ACTIONS

accept	dare	Inflame	reject
adhere	dazzle	inflate	relax
admit	defend	ingratiate	remind
admonish	deflate	inquire	repel
affirm	defy	inspire	reprove
alarm	delay	insult	repulse
allure	delight	intimidate	resist
analyze	demand	intrigue	respect
appeal	demonstrate	introduce	respond
appease	derail	irritate	restrain
approve	devastate	justify	reveal
arouse	dismiss	laugh at	rouse
ask	dispute	like	scar
aspire	distract	love	scold
assail	dominate	lure	seduce
assault	embarrass	manipulate	shame
attack	embolden	marshal	shape
awaken	encourage	mock	share
bait	entice	motivate	shock
beg	entreat	mystify	snatch
beguile	exalt	nullify	soothe
belittle	excite	oblige	stab
beseech	expose	oppose	stalk
bewitch	face up	order	stem
blame	flatter	pacify	stir
blast	follow	patronize	stun
bombard	frighten	persuade	subdue
bruise	get in bed	placate	supplicate
cajole	goad	plead	surmount (overcome)
capture	guide	please	sustain
caution	harass	plot	survive
challenge	hassle	praise	tantalize
charm	have fun	predict	taunt
coax	heal	prevail	tease
comfort	hold up	probe	tempt
command	humiliate	proclaim	terrify
compromise	humor	promise	test
confess	hurt	protect	threaten
confound	illustrate	protest	thrill
confront	impale	provoke	titillate
conquer	impassion	pry	torment
contest	implore	push	tranquilize
control	impress	quash	trust urge on
criticize	incite	question	vilify (speak ill of)
crush	induce	quieten	
		reassure	
		reflect	

TO EDUCATE   TO COACH   TO EMPOWER

www.AIDAacting.com

It's often good to think "What does my character want in this scene?" Or what is my character's opinion or attitude in this scene? You can determine their opinion or attitude from the script, but if you choose a want; here's a few to consider.

WANTS

(Separate from the text, hard to achieve, and you want it off or you are doing it to - the other person)

TO THE OTHER PERSON	FROM THE OTHER PERSON
Belittle	Acceptance
Convince	Affection
Control	Affirmation
Deceive	Appreciation
Dominate	Attention
Humiliate	Be desired
Hurt	Be held
Influence	Commitment
Intimidate	Compassion
Kill	Confession
Make the other person laugh	Confirmation
Manipulate	Cooperation
Provoke	Empathy
Resist	Encouragement
Reject	Forgiveness
Seduce	Freedom
Strike fear	Friendship
	Happiness
	Honesty
	Intimacy
	Love
	Lust
	Peace
	Pity
	Power
	Recognition
	Remorse
	Respect
	Revenge
	Satisfaction
	Sex
	Submission
	Sympathy

To Coach - To Educate - To Empower

It is often good to think "What does my character want in this scene?" Or "What is my character's opinion or attitude in this scene?" You can determine their opinion or attitude from the script. Simply read the script, then make them up. In class I supply my students with a list of wants for them to consider.

For the *want* choice, I would like you to think, "The want that I choose should be separate from the text, hard to achieve, and off or to the other character".

Risk-taking

Risk-taking is an over-used expression that I find is constantly used by entertainment industry people, including teachers.

Many entertainment industry people talk about *risk-taking* in the context of what actors should do. Often you will hear, "I love his work. He's a risk-taker". Yet when you ask that person, "What is a risk?" they may reply, "Oh I don't know", or "I just know it when I see it".

Risk-taking comes in two categories: verbal and non-verbal communication.

When Jack Nicholson's character puts his axe and head through the door in the film *The Shining and says "Here's Johnny!"*, it was a verbal risk as this text was not in the script. When Robert De Niro's character in *Taxi Driver* stands in front of a mirror and says, "You talking to me, you talking to me . . . who the hell you talking to", it was a verbal and non-verbal risk. It was not in the script. When Tom Cruise puckers his lips, like a kiss, at Jack Nicholson in a scene in the courtroom confrontation/climax of the film *A Few Good Men*, it was a non-verbal risk.

I constantly teach actors to take risks. I work with actors on both the verbal and the non-verbal. As silly as it sounds, simply grunting, or whistling on a line or moving towards the other person in the scene, could be a risk. As this type of behaviour is not what you would normally have done in those circumstances. It was unexpected.

Add some to your work and see how the work changes. See how your work can come to life by risk-taking. Below is a list of verbal and non-verbal risks. Feel free to practise them when doing a scene.

Verbal risks

- Drunk
- Raising your volume
- Changing your tone
- Changing the sound of your voice
- Change your accent
- Changing the pace
- Playing with the use of breath
- Play the wants, opinions or attitudes
- Laugh
- Sigh
- Gasp
- Be hysterical
- Stutter or stammer through the line – for example, actors: Hugh Grant, Helen Hunt, Rob Morrow
- Whisper
- Groan
- Whistle
- Say their name
- Sing a line
- Repeat a line
- Emphasis on certain line
- Play opposite the script
- Play surprises
- Be emotional
- Impersonation – for example, Groucho Marx

Non-verbal risks

- Drunk
- Have a headache
- Physical greeting – high 5
- Limp
- Kiss the partner
- Use of kung fu
- Touch the partner
- Laugh
- Sigh
- Try to get something out of your eyes
- Touch yourself in some way
- Play the wants. Going for them. Or for your opinion or attitude
- Distract someone for effect
- Caress
- Cry
- Hug
- Lean on the other person
- Change direction of eyes, head and body
- Grit your teeth as you talk
- Use body in opposite way to dialogue
- Follow/copy the other actor's movements
- Smell someone
- Shiver

I think it is important for you as an actor to work on risk-taking because it helps you become more watchable. It helps you explore the text, the relationship between you and the other characters and helps you create interesting things with the use of your body and voice.

Just as importantly, this helps your exploration of your subtext, that is, what you actually *want* in the scene.

How I incorporate verbal and non-verbal risks into an actor's work is my challenge initially. But it soon becomes the work and actions of the actor.

I teach risk-taking by isolating each verbal and non-verbal risk from the risk lists above. I get actors to initially explore them through improvisation. Firstly, with themselves and then with other actors. Then with text and eventually with whole scenes or scripts or plays.

If we can put the actor in a position where they can isolate these verbal and non-verbal risks and encourage them to explore, then their overall work will be better for it. It is worth noting that this is not always easy to do, and often takes the skill of a teacher or director and the trust and participation of the acting student.

Some human beings don't want to try something new or are afraid of trying something new. So, it is easier to not face their fear, or not to do something they have never done, than it is to take the risks and start exploring.

The rewards for verbal and non-verbal risk-taking are great. I encourage each and every actor to start exploring the above list.

Once the actor starts attaching the verbal and non-verbal risks to a character and scene, they can, subtly or profoundly, change the work they're doing in the scene just by taking the risks.

This works very well for actors who say, "I don't know what to do with my body or my voice". And let's face it, all actors can grow with constant practice with their body and voice.

The smart actor works on verbal and non-verbal risks in class and at home. Then starts putting the risks into their audition work and their professional work.

A note on this: it is important to think of risks and even rehearse risks while rehearsing a scene. But when it is time to *perform live* or *in the camera take*, let it go. See if you can still do it, see if it still comes up. Try not to focus all your time in your mind thinking, "Oh, when she does this, I'll do that", in the scene, because if you do, you will be trying too hard to control the scene.

This is another reason why acting is hard. Because we make premeditated choices and then we have to let them go and do them hopefully *live* or *in the take* and yet try to make the risks look natural and not contrived. This takes practice and more practice.

In addition, by putting yourself in a position to take risks, always listen like a hawk as you interact. Move and be influenced by what the other person or people are doing and saying to *you*. This is so important, as some actors get so caught up with what they're doing sometimes, that they don't let themselves be influenced by the little nuances of human behaviour from others. Such as: a change of tone towards you on a certain line. Be alert. Listen. Take risks. Interact.

There is a very strong correlation between risk-taking and improvisation. This is why improvisation and risk-taking are such good topics to work on. They teach the actor to be affected, as in life, by what comes at you both physically and verbally. Thus, improvisation will definitely help with your risk-taking.

Reflections

During training and before and after auditions, it's a good idea to reflect on what you have done or are doing. That way, you will be able to see if you have done the work required and identify any areas for improvement. Ask yourself the following questions.

During or beforehand

- Did I do relaxation/breath/voice work?
- How am I feeling in my body?
- How am I feeling in my mind?
- Wants... which ones work for me?
- Dropping In The Text layers – did I do them?
- Actions – which ones work for me?
- Did I explore with wants?
- Did I develop rituals? What were they?
- Did I do or consider doing the self-hypnotherapy exercise?

- Did I work with a teacher/coach to help me?

Afterwards

- How was my concentration?
- Did I listen brilliantly?
- Did I tap into one of the five senses at the start of the scene or have a moment before at the beginning? What was it?
- Did I take risks? If so, what verbal and what non-verbal risks did I take?
- Was there a lack of vanity in my work?
- As the scene was about to start, did I let go and explore?
- Did I look at the other person and say: "I want this . . . from you" in your mind
- Did I perform too big?
- Did I perform too small?
- What was the difference between the first take and the second take?
- Did I make a conscious effort to play surprises? What were they?
- What did I think of when I was given direction?
- How did I deal with other actors and their wants?
- Did I self-sabotage at all? If so – how?
- Did I have fun?
- Did I try too much or too hard?
- While acting, was I sitting in the audience or on my own shoulder watching myself act?
- Did I connect with the work?
- Did I play against the script?
- Overall, how do I think I went?
- Did I reward myself afterwards? You should
- Was my acting performance art? Did I explore, explore, explore and not try to nail it

Things to avoid doing

Following is a list of some of the things I have, unfortunately, experienced from actors over my years of teaching since 1990. Fortunately, these comments and/or ways of behaviour are not the norm and came from only a few people.

- What I'm doing is good work in class, why are you not rewarding it? (The teacher thinks that the actor's work is not that good.)
- I've done that month of classes, so I don't need to do it again, ever!
- I don't want to do anything that is not on camera. (Sadly, some actors feel they will become Meryl Streep or Jack Nicholson just from cold reading scenes on camera every week.)
- I'm blaming you, the teacher, for everything that goes on, including my scene partner, for not doing their homework or turning up for class
- I am not going to work on loosening my jaw because by working on exercises by lifting my facial muscles up, it may age me or give me wrinkles
- Going to the gym and working out is more important than working on my acting skills
- I'll turn up to class when I want to
- I'll consistently turn up late to class
- I'll consistently push you to help get me get representation even when I'm not ready for representation
- I don't care how much you give of yourself to me, I want more and if I don't get work, I'll blame you
- Demanding. I'm better than these people in class, so move me to a stronger class (The teacher thinks that this individual is not a better actor.)
- I'm leaving the school because I want the scene to go this way and you wanted it go another way
- I forget what you did for me and I do not thank my teacher or the school

- I don't need any repetition. I want everything new and different every time I come to class

A few reasons why repetition is good

Repetition. Repetition. Repetition. Repetition is an important part of being an actor. The ability to repeat the same thing is an important skill for the actor to have.

Yul Brynner played the King in the musical *The King and I* on Broadway in New York for years. That is, eight shows a week for probably forty-five to forty-six weeks in a year. He did this for years.

In support of this, I have been on film sets where I have had to re-do the same acting scene, over and over, take after take, due to direction, or the weather, or the outdoor lighting, or for some other technical or creative reason.

From time to time, actors will come up against the same learning objectives that they have already completed as part of a curriculum. While every attempt is made to teach the actor as many topics as possible, actors may have to redo a class on a certain topic from time to time, to build on what they have already done. It is actually good for them to do so.

This is where repetition comes in. I encourage all actors to build on what they have learnt the first time in a particular course on a subject. They should not see it as a negative thing.

For example, playing surprises on camera is not easy. Working on passing the baton, listening, and going for your want with a strong colour needs practice. By repeating, let's say, an *On-camera Stage One* class, for example, see it as a perfect way in which to practise your skills to see that you can be better the second time around. More on these things, in detail, in my second book.

An aside: In some other well-known, full-time acting schools in Australia, the actor works on things like movement, breath, and voice work, five days a week for a lot of the first year of their training. Hence, this supports the fact that as an actor, repetition, repetition, repetition is good.

Impulse and non-impulse work

The ability to read people eventually becomes instinctual. For example, a baby that cannot talk realises one day that by crying out he can get attention. The baby uses this device, shall we say, as a form of communication. Of course, he also sees and experiences the result; which is getting attention.

I would like to give you another example on the same thought. Most people develop the ability to read people most of the time, and it eventually becomes instinctual.

Our parents are the people who can affect us the most with what they say and how they say it, and affect us with their body language. Our siblings and partners follow. Based on years of interaction, nobody knows us better than our parents and our siblings who grew up with us. So, they can *push our buttons* in ways far greater and far deeper than anybody else that we interact with. This is because it is learned behaviour, based on memory.

To link these thoughts with acting, when we watch actors who are good at improvising with one another, on stage or screen, why is their work so good?

The simple answer is because each one of them does not know what is going to be said next. Or how it is going to be said. Meaning, how their voice and body is going to change as they work opposite one another.

When actors learn lines and perform a scene, interacting with others, they often forget to really listen to the way the words are being said to them. They fail to notice the changes in the pitch, the volume, and the tone of the voice. The same can be said by the use of someone else's body language being displayed or coming out towards them; through their gestures. They often miss the subtleties of the person opposite them.

As a consequence, they do not show us this *nuance* of human behaviour. That of being in a relaxed open place to be *affected* or *moved* verbally.

Australian actor and acting coach Lindy Davies introduced me to something called *impulse work*. I adapted what was taught to me and call it non-impulse work. This exercise, when done correctly, puts the actors into a situation in which they are asked to give themselves as much time as possible to both say a line and receive a line.

When I say *as much time as possible,* I mean enough time to think of all the ways that you can say what you are about to say, and all the different meanings behind what you are about to say, and all the different thoughts on what is going on with both the situation and what is said to you.

By thinking about this, you then think, what are all the different ways you could interpret what is said to you, including *how* it is said to you, as all of this can be interpreted too.

American actors generally love this non-impulse exercise that I teach, and I think they do because so many of them have had Sanford Meisner training. This exercise has correlations with Meisner technique because it is slow, focused, repetitive and methodical. In this instance, it is repetitive in the mind but not aloud.

Having said that, sometimes I do this exercise with the actors speaking their thoughts aloud. This helps the actors understand the exercise.

Let me describe this exercise. Two actors sit opposite one another with their scene in their hands. With their knees touching, or almost touching, they look at each other as they go through the script.

The actor with the first line thinks about the line and all the ways in which it can be said. When they are ready, they say the line to the other actor. Softly.

The other actor in turn receives the line and takes all the time that is necessary to interpret all the ways they can receive that line; as said above.

They then, in turn, look at their own next line and think of all the ways it can be said. When they are ready, they then speak their next line to their partner. The two actors proceed through the scene at their own pace doing this for each line.

The most important thing with this exercise is to *explore* and consider all the different options as the other actor speaks to you. *Also explore* what you say, and how you say it, and all the different options that it could mean.

The reason this exercise is so powerful is because there is a correlation with this exercise and with what we do in our normal everyday lives. Think back to the baby exercise, where a baby, through *learned behaviour* knows how to get what it wants. As said, parents and siblings will have more impact on you because they know you so well and know how to push your buttons instinctively. This is why this exercise works so well.

People in everyday life don't know what you're going to say and how you're going to say it. They don't know you and your body language intimately, and as a consequence, they cannot instinctively read you unless they know you very well. Well, what if you can have this openness and freshness as an actor? You will be extremely watchable if you can do this.

I want to spell out clearly the beauty of this *non-impulse work.* Because I don't want you to catch the impulse to speak; rather, I want you to take your time and explore.

As an actor, put yourself in a place where you are influenced by the slightest change of volume, tone or pitch, as well as body language, and consider all the different options of what is said and what it means, and how you feel as you are doing the exercise.

This exercise teaches you to be observant, to be an excellent listener, to connect with the other actor and to discover; as opposed to *acting per se.* Being acutely aware of what is happening in a scene and responding emotionally, especially in the eyes or with the tone of the voice, where you might stop blinking, or blush, or cry or scratch your face, is what I call a *nuance of human behaviour*. This sort of work is done very well by strong theatre actors and, in particular, very good film and television actors.

I spend a lot of my time as a teacher training actors in the *nuances of human behaviour* to help them book feature film work in particular. And students do. Give it a go. And remember not to rush the non-impulse exercise; take your time. Also remember, it is an exercise in the training of the actor, not a performance.

A note: It is not uncommon that a three-page scene could take twenty minutes to do the non-impulse exercise.

> ### *Learning Point Number Seventeen*
> - How can you stand out? This chapter sets out a preferred way of thinking and a preferred way of acting through risk-taking.
> - It also gives you a sample script for Dropping In The Text and encourages you to do the non-impulse exercise to help bridge the gap between some ways of human behaviour and communication in life, and your ways of acting as an actor.

Chapter 13
You

In this chapter I would like to talk about you. What is your uniqueness? How well do you present to people? Are you aware of your energy or your aura? Are you healthy? Do you eat well?

What makes you unique?

What is unique about you? An interesting question, isn't it? I remember struggling to think of how to answer that question when asked in my early twenties by casting directors, agents and teachers.

The problem was, I could not *see* the things that were right in front of me. I couldn't see the things that I was thinking and doing which helped define who I was.

If you can relate to this in some way, perhaps you could do the following things to help you see your uniqueness:

- Write down the things you like to do. For example, reading, watching movies, playing a particular sport, dating men or women
- As an actor, be really honest about what you do play well – the comic, the caring friend, the bastard, and so on
- Ask your family and friends to write a few phrases describing you
- Ask your family and friends what characters and occupations they think you look like you could play
- Write a list and then work on these characters

When you get auditions for these types of characters, you have something to draw on. Think, how does a *nurse* hold herself, what is her posture? Or, how does a *truck driver* look? How is their posture? What is the general look on their face? How does their voice sound? Are they unshaven? What type of clothes do they wear?

Creating characters that are your brand will help you get work. To help you get auditions and work, thinking what is unique about you will help you get a better sense of who you are, as well as your strengths, and how other people see you. These things will also help you with your focus to get your big break, or any break for that matter. It is also important because it helps you learn to *market* yourself.

Are you watchable?

As discussed earlier, why would an audience want to watch you? Why would we listen to you?

We are tired, we've worked all day; what is stopping us from falling asleep in the cinema or theatre while watching you perform?

It is really important for you to answer this question – *Why are you watchable?*

Here is an example of an answer to the above question:

I will be so powerful on stage because every word is important to me and so the audience will want to hear my journey. For example, I will connect with my text and go on this journey of discovery with my character and be moved emotionally, and I will explore my relationships with other characters and as a consequence, the audience will explore this too.

Thinking and acting like this will absolutely help you start to understand, develop and market yourself and your uniqueness.

How best to present yourself to industry

As an actor, I got better at presenting myself to industry – casting directors, agents, managers, producers – after I worked on my performance anxiety with a performance anxiety psychiatrist. After a few consultations, I remember him saying to me, "There's nothing wrong with you. You don't need any medication. You simply need to work on why you get performance anxiety".

I used to be so sensitive that if a casting director spoke quickly to me (it could have been because they were behind time in a casting audition),

I used to get affected. My presentation to them and performance were negatively affected.

In addition, if a casting director or other industry person asked me many questions about the work on my résumé, I used to think, "They don't believe that I have done all this work".

I also used to sacredise industry people, especially the casting director, and the role or the show I was going for – in one case, a six-month contract role on the Australian television show *Neighbours*. I also used to think sometimes, "It is about time that you got me in here to audition for you".

These were all very silly things to do or think. If you are reading this and thinking, you are sensitive too and you can relate to some of these things, then try to get over them as soon as you can. In presenting yourself to industry, try to always do it professionally and in the best light.

While living in Los Angeles, I consistently heard from actors who were given opportunities for work because of the people they had met. Actors also got opportunities for work and for theatrical and commercial representation, including from managers, from the people they met and/or were referred to by other people.

In support of this, my eldest brother Colin Parker, who was a very successful salesman in business, once said to me, "People buy people". What this means is that people buy people they like, can trust and they feel can help them achieve their goals in some way. So they pay for their services. "People *buy* people" – it's true.

So, the way you present yourself in the industry is so important because managers, agents and even casting directors, are thinking the following kinds of questions:

- Is this actor a nice person?
- How can I market this actor?
- Do I think there is a need in this industry for this type of actor?
- What is different about this actor?

- Do I want to work with this actor?
- Is this the next movie star?
- How can I cast them, and should I?
- Do they look like they will create interesting characters?
- Do they look like they will understand the story or be able to create their own background story?
- Will they fit in with the current cast?
- Will they be able to handle challenging locations and long hour day challenges?

If you come across as negative, difficult to work with, bland, having no personality, suffer from the *poor me syndrome* or the *I deserve this syndrome,* you will be sending a negative message to that industry or casting person. And you will most likely not be given a job and not be helped in your acting journey.

Bring out your personality

What is your personality like? How can you present you? Some people find it difficult when asked to just be themselves or to explain things about how they are different from other people.

Some actors say, "I'll be whatever you want me to be. I'm an actor". But when you are meeting industry people, they often want to get a sense of who *you are*. If you have a good sense of who you are and where you are going, that will more likely help you.

Try to bring out your own personality. To help you determine who you are, so you can present yourself in the best light, think of your values, things you like and don't like; think of jokes you like, food you like to eat, film/theatre shows you like or attend; think of jobs you have, who your family is, where you come from, what you do on the weekend when you stop working, who are you keeping company with; think of instruments you play, music you like, places you like to travel to, books you like to read, sports you like to play or watch, etc.

If you could write on a piece of paper the answers to all of these questions and keep them with you and have them fresh in your mind, this will help you with being able to present yourself in the best light when you present yourself to industry.

Metaphysics and you

What do you know about metaphysical energy? Have you ever thought that energy surrounds you? Are you aware of your aura? Are you aware of other people's auras? Do you read about metaphysical energy? Do you know that we all give off energy, both positive and negative? Do you try to permeate positive energy? If you don't, I think you should.

I like to work with actors and teach them about metaphysical energy and auras. I won't go into much detail on metaphysics and auras, as there are many books out there that do deal with these topics. I teach a class in which I cover actors' energy and auras, as well as how to present themselves through their energy in their best light. Please excuse the pun.

Here is an example on how I do this: in one class I worked with actors asking them to relax their mind, bodies and souls. I asked them to close their eyes and breathe down into their bodies and feel what it is like to notice and acknowledge all the different parts of their bodies. For example, their feet touching the ground, the gentle movements of the body, how the spine is holding the body and neck and head up, and so on.

I then asked the actors to ask for some sort of universal support. To feel the light, a kind of calming white or blue or yellow light on them. This could be God or Jesus Christ or some other religious support. Or a family member, partner, friend or loved one. As long as they felt they were in tune with themselves and felt that they were being supported and welcomed into the universe in some way. I know it sounds corny to some people, but simply thinking of having some support seems to help us all feel connected and more open, and free and most importantly here, in a position to try to feel other people's energy and see their auras.

I then asked the actors to open their eyes and to try to be still, stay natural, neutral, non-judgmental and to move around the space feeling open and to move to people that they felt have positive energy. Or an energy of a person that they felt attracted to.

This exercise is so interesting as, in this and many other classes, actors generally all gravitated to the same one or two or three people.

I then moved onto doing acting exercises beginning with sounds and movements with actors responding to them. It was just two lines from the start of a scene, and I asked the actors to work with many people delivering the text, slowly moving from one actor to another, and then choosing who they felt they had the strongest connection with.

Above: Paul feeling the lovely energy from friends at an industry event at the Sky Bar on the Sunset Strip in Hollywood in 2019.

This last part is very important. Actors generally had a terrific time of discovery doing this exercise. This is because they were feeling drawn to some actors more than others. They were feeling connected to some actors more than others and consequently they were having deeper connections with some more than others.

I talked to the actors about the fact that this is the sort of connection casting directors, directors and producers are looking for from actors.

A chemistry or connection between actors, when they read opposite them, or a connection or chemistry when actors read in pairs or with already cast actors in film, television, theatre and commercials.

Casting directors, producers and directors often want the auditioning actor to quickly create chemistry or some sort of connection. So, you have to ask yourself, what is your ability to connect with other people like? How are you connecting with others? Because if you are connecting with others on a deep level, well, that is very interesting to watch and this will help you get cast.

As interesting as this exercise sounds, I like to conclude work on this topic in class by asking actors to vote on the people with whom they felt the strongest connections.

The people most chosen were always voted for by a lot of actors in the class, and were actors who booked the most work.

No surprises here for me. But certainly interesting for the actors to all see and experience. At the other end of the scale, actors with very few or no votes also generally seemed to be the actors who struggled to get work or representation.

Their energy, their aura and most importantly, their ability to make connections with others, were not on as deep a level as others in the class. Coincidence? I don't think so. Profound stuff indeed? Yes, it is.

A final word on this topic: have some stories to tell industry people, humorous, light stories. So that when asked you have something light or humorous to talk about. I suggest you write down three short stories and familiarise yourself with them.

Again, if you come across as negative, difficult to work with, or have no personality and suffer from the *poor me syndrome* or the *I deserve this syndrome*, you will have negative energy and you will be sending a negative message to that casting person, agent, manager, producer or director. The consequences will then most probably be that you are less likely to make a positive impression, be helped or represented.

Your diet

I have taught many actors who have been heightened by power drinks, energy drinks, soda and caffeine drinks and, unfortunately, some other *uppers* to give them energy. Generally, their concentration and listening was affected in a negative way. It showed in their eyes and behaviour – such as *their* listening. Eat and drink wisely, your mind and body *are* your tools.

I myself am a bowel cancer survivor. I was diagnosed with bowel cancer in my tenth year of living in the USA. Nowadays my family and I do our best to eat well. My diet is mixed Japanese and Australian (Australian is basically international/British cuisine).

A balanced diet, a balanced exercise program and a calm and peaceful mind are all good starting points for the actor.

We are what we eat. I'm sure you have heard this cliché before. Well, it's true: what you eat and drink will profoundly affect you, your health, concentration, energy levels, digestive system and acting.

Drinks containing caffeine (especially coffee), energy drinks and soft drinks/sodas containing sugar, corn syrup and high fructose corn syrup will all affect your ability to concentrate as they are non-natural uppers.

These uppers could and often do affect an actor's concentration and listening skills. So, be careful before taking a lot of caffeine, sugar or corn syrup prior to going to class, an audition or on set.

I have included this basic information about diet because I want you to live a happy and healthy life. And also because poor eating and drinking affects your concentration, ability to listen and energy levels. All the things an actor has to have going well.

Learning Point Number Eighteen

- Who are you and what do you do?
- Try to get to know your uniqueness, your eating habits and focus on being grounded, centred and healthy.
- Also work on your energy. Your metaphysical energy.

Conclusion
What I won't do (other teachers shouldn't either)

In my teaching of actors, I have not and do not do the following:

- Would not stand you there and strip you down and abuse or insult you. Drawing attention to your height, weight, appearance or talent. Or abuse the choices you make as an actor
- Would not sit there and chain smoke in front of the class, giving you all the possibility of second-hand lung cancer
- Would not sit out alone, like on a pedestal, separate from everyone else, pretending that I am greater than everyone else and "untouchable" as an acting coach
- Would not name drop or write a book that name drops famous actors' names in every chapter
- Would not ask personal questions about your own life and then use the personal questions against you. By throwing them back into your face to try to get a response from you, that you seem to not be able to give as an actor
- Would not pretend to know it all, or threaten to throw you out of class for asking lots of questions
- Would not have any class objectives, lesson plans or curriculum
- Would not teach you some external eye-flipping exercise to cause the eye to go red and weep. I've been told some teachers tell actors to do this to bring on the tears.
- Would not get you to stand face on, very close to a wall, and tell you to yell at yourself until you're exhausted. Telling you that this is the way to get emotional as an actor

What I will do in my teaching of actors

- Train you to cry on cue and be able to assess your emotions with breath and chakra alignment exercises. In other words, an organic and human body physiological way of obtaining emotion
- Teach you to act and encourage you to believe in yourself when training you
- Teach you how to connect breath, thought, image and voice to be more believable as an actor
- Teach you to approach performing as an actor coming from love and not fear
- Teach you that you should explore and not try to put pressure on yourself by thinking "I'm going to nail it" in the class, scene, workshop or audition
- Teach you that a relaxed, creative, risk-taking mind, body and spirit will help you produce better work
- Teach you to bring out the warrior within you. A warrior who is strong, courageous, creative and able to stand challenges and overcome them
- Teach you to develop personal independence and empowerment, so your life is not guided, influenced or provoked into fear by teachers or daily television news programs, or anyone else for that matter
- Teach you a plethora of options from which to draw. All to help you discover the character, the character's journey and the script's journey overall
- Teach you that exploring and entering the work with a free, open mind and spirit will bring you to a place where you will continue the journey of discovery during the course of the theatre production or the film/TV shoot
- In conclusion, I teach and the actor prepares. They prepare profoundly. They look at their text and the script's journey and their character's journey and explore as many options as

- possible. Their exploration could include putting different acting techniques into their work, if I, or they, felt the need to do it.
- With this philosophy and way of practising, the actor reaches rehearsal or performance with an open mind. Then they are there, in a position, to continue to explore and discover. The prepared actor that I teach still discovers during performance.
- Always listening, always discovering, always learning. Daniel Day Lewis and Cate Blanchett are two actors that spring to mind who do this extremely well in their work.
- If the actor feels he knows it all, the performance will not have an edge. It will feel lazy, premeditated and perhaps have elements of contrivance. The best metaphor I can think of here is to think of talking to someone in real life: our day is not scripted out for us; it is, in many ways, an improvisation.

In closing, who said acting was easy? Acting isn't easy. I can try to make you great. But no one can be inside your mind or body and control your every move. You yourself have to develop the right thought patterns and train this way or that way, to help you to be in a place of exploration. A place of discovery. A place that is grounded in technique. A place in which to take risks.

You must be prepared to fail. You must communicate well with casting directors, your director/teacher and fellow actors, and you must be in touch with who you are. You should be in touch well enough with yourself to be able to create interesting characters. Watchable characters in your portrayals. This is so because that's your job, personifying other people.

This is again where I would like to draw on the correlation between your personal development and your acting chops – your skills. From personal experience, and from my teachings over many years, I can encourage you to work on the inner you, as well as to implement techniques covered in this book. Especially the breath work, the breath, thought, image, voice connection and the Dropping In The Text techniques. If you find the

Australian techniques work for you, as thousands of people that I have trained have, then great!

Looking back over my career, from the perspective of the older, wiser and more experienced actor that I became in the early 2000s, the more I realised that my anxiety, nervousness, insecurity, paranoia, distrust in myself and lack of belief in the energy of the universe – all of these things affected my presentation of self in casting offices and with the industry at large.

This, of course, was not good for my acting career. And it wasn't just in my acting. Sometimes it was in my private life as well. In hindsight, I discovered that one of the reasons that I became an actor was to seek acceptance and love. I never trusted enough that all the things would come to me if I was in the right state of mind, body and spirit.

I do not want this to happen to you. You, the reader, could be thinking now: "I know where this writer is coming from. He has had personal experiences of things he is explaining here". I have. Most people write about what they know and what they have experienced when writing non-fiction. Fortunately, as of 2021, I have twenty-five years of working as an actor and thirty-two years of teaching experience, to draw from as well.

Many industry professionals have the necessary training, experience and skills to be able to discover the good people, the people in tune with themselves, the people who will work best *in with* a cast and crew on a theatre show or on a set. I want you to be one of those actors! So, please work on the inner you. "Go get 'em" – I like to say.

What I suggest you do is practise the ways of thinking outlined in this book, together with the practical exercises.

One final important note: I am fully aware that I have given you a plethora of things to think about and a kaleidoscope of exercises to work on to help make you a better actor. But what if you don't have the time to do all the things mentioned in your preparation prior to an audition?

Such as, all the layers of the Dropping In The Text technique? The answer is simple: do as much as you can based on your timeframe, prior to the audition or the production; if that is the level that you are at.

Please follow this same principle when working on a television set. Because on a television set, things change really quickly sometimes and you have to learn lines for future episodes between your current takes on set. More on this in book two.

If you are a beginner and not auditioning yet, you will have plenty of time to do all the exercises described in this book.

Learning Point Number Nineteen

- Try to implement these ways of thinking, seeing and behaving.
- Be sure to include the techniques, exercises and rituals. I empower you!

Appendix 1
Handouts

As a teacher, I am very *big* on handouts. Here are some from my school, AIDA, including orientation into the school, creating characters, scene study theory and improvisations rules and tips.

Orientation into the school

AIDA offers a curriculum that is diverse, challenging and has an international flavour. The curriculum has been devised deliberately to give actors all-round training. New students to the school fill out this questionnaire so I can ascertain their goals. I am including it here because it is important for both of us. It is important for you to think this way about your chosen career. It is Show *Business* after all. Think of yourself as a small business. It is important for me because I can get a gage of where you are at of where you want to go and what you want to work on.

Student orientation handout

S.W.O.T. Analysis Of Your Acting Career

- What are your strengths?
  ....
- What are your weaknesses?
  ....
- What are your opportunities?
  ....
- What are your threats?
  ....

Your most important goals as an actor:

1..

2..

3..

4..

5..

What do you see as your biggest career challenges right now? Please list them and be as specific as possible:

....

How do you like to be assessed? Please check or circle one of the following:

- Strongly
- Firmly
- Gently

By completing the questionnaire prior to commencing class, the actor allows me to see where they're at.

Then together we can work towards getting them better and achieving their goals. These questions also give me an insight into a student's psyche and positivity (or lack of it), as well as allowing me to plan where to guide them first.

I will be talking a lot more about creating characters in book two, but I wanted to give you this list here as it lets you know a variety of ways in which to help you create characters.

Creating characters

Below is a sample of one of the charts that I use to help actors create characters.

Character development chart

Use of body

- Gait, mannerisms

- Affected by: war, pregnancy, emotions/thoughts, occupation, missing limb

Use of voice

- Centre of breath, voice, accent, tone, affectation, volume, pitch, flavour

Use of mind/backstory *(has correlations with Stanislavski technique)*

- Character background information from a Scene Study 1 lesson plan; described in detail in book two
- Your want

Laban influence

- B – Body E – Effort S – Shape S – Space
- Effort dimension – Space, Time, Weight, Flow
- Actions – Punch, Slash, Press, Wring, Float, Glide, Flick, Dab

Animal influence *(has correlations with Grotowski technique)*

- What animal to choose? How does the animal influence the use of the body and the voice?

Imitation *(has correlations with Brecht technique)*

- Copying, imitating someone as best you can
- Drawing attention to what you're doing

Stimuli

- props/costumes, visual images, stream of consciousness, adjectives, observation

Below are some questions the AIDA acting school actor asks themselves to help create background to scene and background to character. If you are given a whole script or play, then you have plenty to draw on, including your research. However, if you only have one scene (scenes are called sides in the USA), then you need to make it up.

An actor with backstory will always give a more fruitful, richer performance than an actor who just tries to wing it. One of the reasons why this is so is because they have made decisions regarding their character in the scene. They have also made decisions about how they their character feels about other characters in the scene.

In support of this, an actor who has created backstory will have made some decisions on how they have considered responding to what is said to them in the scene.

They will have also made some decisions about why they are saying what they are about to say in the scene.

Scene study theory

I will be talking a lot more about scene study in book two, but I wanted to give you these questions below as it encourages you to think and make some backstory decisions. By backstory I mean: you create a history for your character, and background for what has gone on prior to the start of the scene.

To assist your interpretation of a play, script or scene, ask yourself these questions:

What are your immediate thoughts about the play or script or scene?

What is the main statement of the play? Or script? Or scene?

In one sentence, summarise the play, script or scene.

What are the playwright's intentions? Sometimes playwrights write through allegory. The playwright has a story, something that happened to them, or a particularly strong view of a social or political issue and they share it through their play. If you don't know what the story is, take a guess and/or make it up based on what you do know that's been given to you in the scene.

What is the political and social content? What is happening within the play? The playwright links the social and political issues in the script to real life within the play. For example, in *Lord of the Rings* how teamwork is important to achieve a goal and not to give into temptation or evil doings.

What is the political and social context? What is happening outside of the play? What are the similarities between the issues in the scene/play and events happening outside the play in the world today or during that time period? For example, in *Lord of the Rings* – friendship, temptation, pressure of responsibility, leadership, ability to speak up in a workplace, teamwork, good versus evil.

What is the super objective? The bigger picture/philosophical view. For example, in *Lord of the Rings* – goodness will prevail!

What is the spinal objective? What storylines/plots are there? Are they entwined? What thread do you think is running through the whole scene? For example, *Lord of the Rings* – the ring is the spine. We see the ring in a running stream in the opening scene of the first movie, and the ring being dropped in the volcano in the last scene in the final movie.

Character Questions. Overall thoughts of character:

- Who am I?
- Where have I been?
- What place am I in now?
- What is the current time, date and year?
- What am I going to do here?
- What do I want?
- How will I get it?
- What must I overcome?
- Who is here?

- What are the sensory realities of the place that I am in?
  - Sight
  - Taste
  - Sound
  - Smell
  - Touch

Character background charts: Internal and external

Listed below are external and internal background categories to aid you in your development of your characters. I have added some examples to assist you with the categories.

- **Internal – Need**: Desire, want, subtext or another internal stimulus
- **Internal – Social Background:** Religion, where the character comes from, family, status/class
- **Internal – Ethical Values:** Learned behaviour through family/surroundings, values, religious values (e.g. they value marriage, love, code of ethics, they don't kill, they abide by government's laws and society's rules).
- **Internal – Physical Peculiarities:** Age, habits (biting fingernails and lips, twirling hair), twitches, facial features, body features, peculiar expressions, physicality from an accident or birth defect (e.g. limp). Psychological damage could change the physicality (e.g. being yelled at or abused as a child could affect posture and/or the use of the body).
- **Internal – Psychological Peculiarities**: Speech impediments, psychological damage, personality traits, disorders, thoughts and ideas. A physicality could affect the psychological and make one insecure or shy. You do things or say things that could be peculiar and could stem from your thought patterns.
- **External – social environment**: Social class of the environment? e.g. Beverly Hills or South Central in Los Angeles? What's going on in the place, the majority political view of the environment?

(e.g. conservative versus liberal environment). Time period (e.g. modern-day versus Elizabethan). What can you see there? What does the general neighbourhood look like? Are there any hotels? (e.g. city, state, buildings).

- **External – physical environment:** Describe the setting: People in the space, the season, location description of the room and things in it, the date, sensory realities.
- **External – relationships and/or attitudes towards other characters:** Make a decision about who the character is with and how you feel about them. Age? Why you like/dislike them? How long have you known them? How do you know them, etc.?
- **External – specific given circumstances:** The most important things you want to note from the scene. List them.

Improvisation tips list

This list was compiled by my students and me in classes. Improvisation is important to the actor to:

- help you build a character
- help you trust your peers who you work with. This builds atmosphere and relationships with other people and other characters
- help you uncover the subtext of a scene
- open up your creative mind and senses
- help with auditions and re-direction, especially in commercials or when someone forgets a line
- help you have the ability to respond to the unexpected
- help you listen
- help keep you in the moment
- encourage you to take risks
- help you use your body more in a scene
- help you be more flexible with interpretations of text and character which help you make choices to build confidence as a performer
- make it more likely that you will go with what is given to you in a scene, as well as given to you from another person

- have fun

Improvisation rules

Remember: LID Listen - Invent - Don't block

Remember: the ACTION – create – support – add - conclude

This list of rules below was also compiled by my students and me in classes.

- Give and take between people
- Pay attention to the circumstances
- Don't put the "success" of the improvisation all on the other person
- Be prepared to relinquish pre-conceived choices or ideas as you enter the space. In other words, allow yourself to be changed
- Use the space (environment)
- Don't talk over one another
- Follow your impulses
- Trust each other
- Think ensemble and not monologue
- Physically work in with your peers
- Have fluid transitions within the scene
- Stay in the moment/story
- Don't dominate the scene
- Everyone participates
- Have an arc – a beginning, middle and an end
- Don't leave the space without justifying
- Adhere to Paul Parker's "The Action" (as described earlier and below)
- If it gets stale, change it
- If in a group of four, remember four brains are better than one
- Be uninhibited
- Establish who you are and your relationship with others as soon as possible
- Establish the environment

- Establish where you've just come from
- Commit to what's been given
- Commit to the character and the other actors and the scene
- Listen like a hawk
- Don't hit or grab anyone
- Be in the proper neutral position
- Don't distract others while in neutral position
- Tell a story
- If you are a non-speaker in a group improv, assist the progression or conclusion of it
- Go with the flow, whatever is said
- Consider the possibility of going against the norm
- Don't alter a character's personality mid-improvisation
- Don't ignore what's going on around you
- Try to always face the audience. Don't show your back. Align yourself with other actors. No upstaging
- Don't ask questions early on. Make statements
- Abstain from being bossy and assigning other people their roles
- Acknowledge imaginary objects
- Be truthful in the scene
- Trust the scene and your peers
- If you establish a role or format, stick to it (subject to qualification)
- Don't perform for the laugh
- Do perform for the laugh
- What you create, talk about, discuss and have it between you and others, not off the stage. In other words, don't talk about people or things that are happening elsewhere. Make the story about the people and what is going on right there in front of the audience
- Try to speak and move with a purpose
- You don't have to talk
- Speak clearly so you're understood
- You can be an inanimate object
- Use your imagination
- Don't judge yourself or your peers

- Don't be afraid to add more people to the scene
- Practise stage blocking, so you know what it is and what not to do. "Blocking" in this context meaning, positioning on stage and not upstaging anyone

The drama

- Drama is the give and take between people
- Create a scenario
- Make it interesting
- Create conflict without blocking. "Blocking" in this context meaning, without saying no
- Create characters and establish the situation/surroundings
- Have a drama/conflict
- Move the drama forward. Resolve or bring the drama to a conclusion
- Have surprises
- Have a climax/peak
- Have an arc: a beginning, middle and end
- Have a journey
- Have or create a plot
- Have variable opinions
- Clever is good
- React to the drama
- Don't be afraid to be emotional
- Don't play it for laughs, play it for real
- Raise the stakes
- Be in relationship with your partner (have a connection)
- Put a character in a position of change
- Feel free to change your status

The Action – *in a group of four actors*

- Create – 1st actor makes sure the story is started
- Support – 2nd actor makes sure the story is supported
- Add – 3rd actor makes sure the story has an add onto the story
- Conclude – 4th actor makes sure the story is finished

The humour

- Be truthful and humour will come
- Have energy and commitment to character
- Timing – alter your pace with delivery
- The unexpected is good
- Bait and switch (set something up, then do the opposite)
- Humour is what you and others think people will laugh at
- Physical comedy
- Make fun of yourself
- Try to find the humour
- Imitate people/celebrities
- Exaggerate the characteristics
- Deliver the three-line set-up (each comment is more ridiculous and an exaggeration of the last comment)
- Don't try to be funny
- Play off other people
- Physicality/sarcasm/faces is good
- Don't often enter with preconceived ideas
- It is good to play or say opposite what we think you will say or do
- It is good to have humour
- Deliver the absurd with straight delivery
- Play opposite the text
- Try to surprise people and yourself
- Add sound effects

The fun

- Enjoy the improvisation
- Be spontaneous
- Smile, it will help
- Go along for the ride
- Use child-like imagination. Don't be afraid
- Don't criticise yourself
- Don't force it
- Remember to have fun – an audience knows
- Put yourself into it
- Relax and breathe
- Don't be safe – take a risk
- Don't care what you do
- Be silly
- Tap into the audience's energy
- Have lots of energy
- Don't be hindered by reality
- Watch cartoons and read
- It is okay to be stupid

Above: Paul preparing a lesson plan for the AIDA school.

Appendix 2
Lesson plans

In this section, I would like to give you a sample of a lesson plan. This is because non-educational people often do not know what a curriculum is or what a lesson plan is or what class objectives are.

As I've said in this book, lesson plans come from a school's curriculum. The curriculum comes from the philosophy, vision, mission statement and general methods of instruction within a particular teaching body; in this case, my AIDA acting school. A curriculum could also include the influences and requirements from an educational government body.

As said, I am a strong believer in lesson plans: the teacher plans for the teaching lesson. AIDA's lesson plans come from my curriculum. The lesson plans have each class's learning objectives clearly listed. Sometimes these objectives are listed for the student to see.

Hence, I often tell the students the lesson plan's objectives for each class. I also sometimes provide a handout with the assessment criteria for each lesson's objectives.

All good teachers should leave room to improvise and digress from the lesson plans. This is because things will undoubtedly come up in class that you didn't expect. It is really important for the teacher to address those things and digress for a moment or two, to make some other points, or let some other things in class evolve.

The following information is part of a lesson plan. It is taken from the first page of my Australian Techniques 1 Lesson Plan, part of my curriculum. My curriculum has levels: level 1, level 2, and so on. Many subjects that I teach have four levels. Australian Techniques has eight levels.

Level One: Australian Techniques 1

For a group class this consists of four classes of three hours duration over four weeks with one class a week. Preferably on the same day or night of the week. The aim is to help the actor create a technique ritual of studying to improve their acting skills.

Student preliminary work: before the first class starts, students are to bring a printed short monologue of their choice to class. A monologue that they have never done before. Preferably with emotion in it. A dramatic monologue. Not Shakespeare or Ancient Greek, and they are not to choose a monologue that they have written themselves. This way we get a new start. If necessary, I can give students a selection of monologues to choose from.

Handouts to be given out over the four weeks:

- S.W.O.T. analysis handout
- Monologue selection, where necessary
- Dropping In The Text – the layering stages handout
- Wants, opinion or attitude handout
- Action handout
- Points of concentration handout
- Chakra chart handout
- Emotional exercise handout

Lesson Plan – Week One

Teacher/lecturer: Objectives of lesson:

- For students to feel comfortable with each other. Initiated through grouped game, warm-up work
- To give students the overall philosophy and principles of what the four-week course is about and what will happen in the classes. For example: The course will end with actors performing a monologue with emotional content and will be given direction and constructive criticism on the students portrayal of the technique taught and on their performance of their piece

- To focus on breath awareness and connection within the body and then to link it with thought, image and voice. Emotion will come naturally
- To put into practice, through exercises, a particular warm-up routine
- To introduce chakra and emotional connection work with breath, voice and body work
- Introduce the "Dropping In The Text" exercises in conjunction with the students' or teacher's monologue
- Explain to students how they will be assessed and what is required of them. Here is a sample: the actors will perform the monologue with the said technique and be directed. The actors should endeavour to connect their text with their breath, their thoughts and images and their voice

Then I would begin the warm-up exercises.

Above: AIDA actors about to start a warm-up exercise in Hollywood.

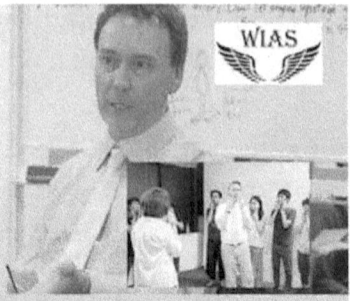

Above: A workshop flyer prepared by the acting school for Paul's teaching in Japan in 2019.

Appendix 3
People who influenced my teachings

I would like to formally thank the following people for their love and support and guidance over the years. A guidance that has helped me write this book.

- My first two drama teachers in high school in Melbourne in the 1970s: Patricia Cornelius, now an established Australian playwright, and Debbie Silverstein
- The late Graeme Bent. A character actor/teacher who I studied with in Russell Street in Melbourne in the late 1970s
- My long-time mentor, actor Reg Evans, who was tragically taken from us in the Black Saturday bushfires of early 2009 in Australia
- At Deakin University/Victoria College-Rusden Campus, lecturers/teachers: Cliff Hadley, Sue Nicholson, Bob Holden, Peter Farago and Yoni Prior
- As well as: Lindy Davies, Bill Pepper, David Latham, Aarne Neeme, Dean Carey, Roger Hodgman and Paul Hampton

The layout and some aspects of **breath, thought, image, voice connection** come from: David Latham of Melbourne and Bill Pepper of Sydney, as well as Kristin Linklater's book *Freeing the Natural Voice*, Drama Publishers, USA, 1976.

The layout and some parts of **Dropping In The Text, chakra alignment** and **emotional exercises** come from: David Latham of Melbourne via Mike Alfreds, Leonard Meenach and Kristin Linklater.

Scene study charts: Lindy Davies of Melbourne and Konstantin Stanislavski.

The initial impulse exercise: Lindy Davies of Melbourne.

Above: A picture from Paul's 2019 teaching tour – teaching in Hollywood. Celebrity actress Jeannetta Arnette is the blonde woman, moving across the stage, front left. Larena Patrick is behind her.

Appendix 4
The AIDA school and successful students

Please allow me to talk a little bit about my school. It is important because my school has an educational focus. My school has a mission statement and principles. My school has a curriculum, areas of study and lesson plans.

Acting begins with breath work and listening. I work to release tension from actors' bodies and open them up to breathe the way they did when they were infants. Or close to it.

During the first months of training, my students begin to learn to experience emotional connection on cue. As the student nears completion of their first level of training, they will be performing scenes and monologues with emotional clarity and honesty. This is only the beginning.

Please see the following sections in this book for guidance and exercises on how to do these things:

- Breath and voice (pages 84 to 87)
- Connecting breath, thought, image and voice (pages 78 to 80)
- Chakra work (page 90)
- Emotional exercises (page 93)
- Dropping In The Text (pages 95 to 102)

My private and class coaching with the AIDA curriculum then moves into providing actors with comprehensive script breakdown and story analysis techniques, as well as neutral mask and movement work.

The AIDA curriculum also includes, on-camera, scene study and improvisation classes. I also incorporate international theorists' work such as Brecht, Grotowski, Lecoq, Laban and Stanislavski. And there are audition preparation and training classes too.

Please see the following sections in this book for guidance and exercises on how to do these things too:

- Scene Study charts (pages 240 to 243)
- Creating characters (pages 238 to 240)
- International theorists (pages 113 to 125)
- Auditioning (pages 127 to 141)
- Improvisation (pages 243 to 248)

At the AIDA school there are many and varied teaching levels, all designed to train the actor. The courses in these levels vary and are designed to give the actor as many skills as possible. Each level I teach has four individual months of classes. All month-to-month classes are four to six weeks of intensive work.

Having taught acting for the screen since 2000, in 2020, the curriculum that I created branched into specialising in *on-camera* classes for performing in the frame and for self-tapes.

I and my staff are proud of the level of care and attention we give our students. Not every actor has the same needs, wants or desires. We always try to listen to our actors. While actors are in our care, we ensure that they are exposed to emotional connection at a level achieved by today's most sought-after actors.

To ensure AIDA actors are getting the most from their tuition, I and the AIDA staff employ these principles:

- PRINCIPLE ONE: We provide well-rounded training of the actor. Not just scene study and cold reading classes
- PRINCIPLE TWO: We are a committed, passionate and caring teaching and administrative ensemble that will guarantee to improve the actor's work
- PRINCIPLE THREE: We take care and attention to every actor and his or her growth through the school

- PRINCIPLE FOUR: A few chosen actors have had the choice of financial incentive group plans
- PRINCIPLE FIVE: The actor can enter the AIDA family that has many school-based and peer group incentives and privileges
- PRINCIPLE SIX: We have a history of empowering our actors. We will continue to propel them into action

At AIDA, we understood that actors' training, careers and career potential are in our hands. We want that. We also want only the best for our students. AIDA is a safe, secure, reliable, experienced international acting school, since 2002.

I know this reads very much like an advertisement for my school. In fact, the above few paragraphs have been taken from one of my school's advertising flyers. I took the time to set out this information for you in this book so you can clearly read that the AIDA school and my curriculum, my teachings and staff have a structure. We have a foundation. We have a purpose. We have principles. We have a focus.

Paul Parker and AIDA's teaching successes

Below is a small list of some of the thousands of actors that I am proud to have trained over the years. Please feel free to put their names into IMDB – the International Movie database at www.imdb.com – to read about their film and television achievements. In case you are unfamiliar with IMDB, web series, commercials and theatre bookings are not listed on IMDB.

USA

- Jeannetta Arnette
- Tarnau Massaquoi
- Elina Madison
- Gerald Webb
- Allison McAtee
- Elisabeth Noone
- Preston Jones

- Naama Kates
- Nicole Dionne
- Chris Ivan Cevic
- Patrick Censoplano
- Michele Massey (Bedell)
- Karnell Matthews
- Bonnie Piesse
- Damaris Diaz
- Robin Leabman
- Jennifer Hutchins
- Perry Wolberg
- Chelsea Taylor
- Yolanda Romersa
- Samantha Carro
- Rebecca Brooks
- Bronwen Masters
- Mary Elisabeth Boylan
- Carolyn Neff
- Adam Jennings
- Emily Roche
- Charles Gorgano
- Tanayi Seabrook
- Cyanne McClairian
- Danielle Vasinova
- Patricia De Leon
- Julie Nesbitt
- Tansy Alexander
- Christine Nguyen
- Benu Mabhena
- Devin Keaton
- Frank Rada
- Mike Larose
- Bart Baggett
- Peta Johnson

- Sara Davenport
- Larena Patrick
- Mitra Hajjar
- Lauren Simon
- Jani Wang
- Cameron Cipolla
- HC Fletcher

Australia

- Ella Newton
- Simone Annan
- Adele Wilson
- Kristen May
- Harrison Popple
- Christopher Erasmus
- Ally Aurora
- Candice Leask
- Gemma Louise Murphy
- Monica Kumar
- Rachael Wegener
- Kat Ludley
- Susie Kazda

Japan

- Kyoko Kudo
- Mika Konada
- Tomoko Ogawa

Appendix 5
Paul Parker full curriculum vitae as teacher/coach

I don't profess to be a celebrity. I am simply a teacher doing my job. However, if I can't list all my credits here in my book – where can I? Please allow me to list them here.

PAUL PARKER, Lecturer/Teacher/Coach/Artistic Director

Paul received a Bachelor of Education in Drama/English from the prestigious Rusden/Deakin University teaching program in Melbourne in 1991. Paul has been teaching, on and off, in Australia since 1990. He started his own acting school, AIDA – Australian Institute of Dramatic Arts International – in 2002.

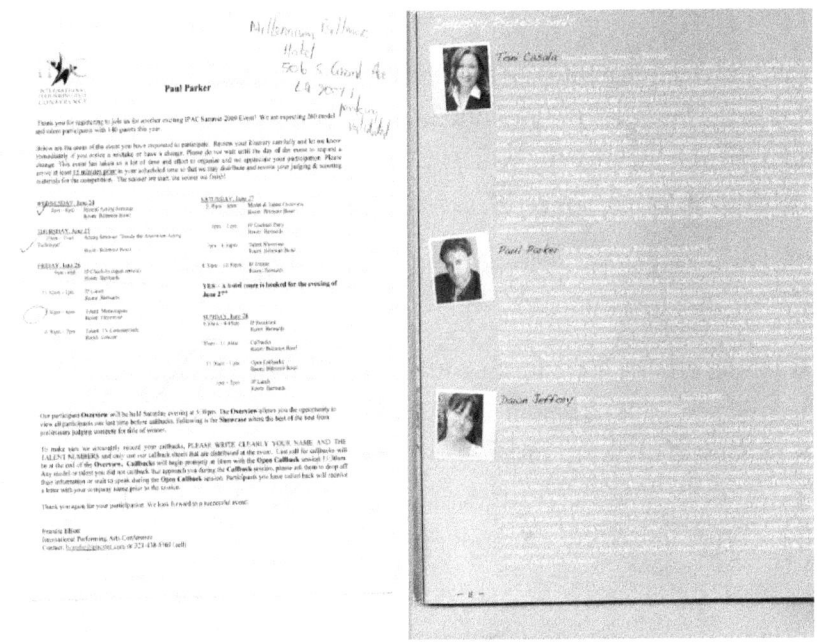

Above: Information from the booklets for the 2009 & 2010 IPAC conferences.

Teaching

Paul has been teaching acting since 1990 and teaching Performance in Business Presentation since 2002. He taught in the USA, on the ground, daily, from June of 2002 to July 2011. Then on teaching tours in 2014, 2015, 2016, 2018 and 2019, as well as online since 2011.

Paul also taught annually in Japan from 2013 to 2019, and taught at Universities in China in 2010.

Teaching credits include: In Australia, Head of Department, Highvale Secondary College; Victorian Arts Centre – Art Education Program; Northern Melbourne Institute of Dramatic Arts (TAFE); Holmesglen Institute of TAFE; Australian College of Dramatic Arts; Deakin University; and SMB – School of Mines & Industries Ballarat (TAFE).

In the USA, founder, teacher/lecturer/coach and Artistic Director of AIDA, current since June 2002; and IPAC – International Performing Arts Conference 2007–10, in Los Angeles and San Francisco.

In Japan, Stone Wings International School (2013–19); Jikei International (2017–16); and Engeki Workshop (2016).

In China, at Geely University, Beijing (2010); and Hainan University Sanya College, Hainan Province (2010).

In Sth Korea, online, since 2021.

In England, online, since 2022.

Directing

Paul has been directing since 1990. Credits in Australia include: working as an Assistant Director to Roger Hodgman at Melbourne Theatre Company in *Lady Windermere's Fan* by Oscar Wilde (with Robyn Nevin, Max Gillies, Gerry Connolly and Frances O'Connor in the cast), and at St. Martins Theatre.

In the USA, Paul directed three AIDA Showcases in 2004, 2005 and 2009 (2009 was a national tour performing in Los Angeles, San Francisco and Off Broadway in New York). Paul also directed eleven comedy review shows in Hollywood from 2005 to 2006 and many AIDA Open house day performances.

Paul directed six short films and numerous student show reels.

Acting

Paul acted from 1977 to 2003. Credits include: Television in Australia – *The Sullivans, Neighbours, Full Frontal, Funky Squad, One Step, Two Step, Tickle Under There*. In the USA – *Young and The Restless* (with Lauralee Bell). Film in Australia – *Eloise* (lead role), *The Elixir* (with Tiriel Mora, Henri Szeps), *Six O'clock Swill* (with Annie Bryon/Jason Clarke), *America – Brick Island*.

Paul also acted in dozens of theatre shows across Melbourne, Sydney and Los Angeles, including at the Adelaide Fringe Festival and the Melbourne International Comedy Festival in Australia. Paul won an NAACP award for Best Actor as a part of Danny Glover/Ben Guillory's Robey Theatre Company's *For the Love of Freedom Part 1* in Los Angeles in 2001 and two television on-screen awards for an Eisteddfod competition in Australia in 1998.

Full listing of Paul Parker's credits as a teacher/coach

- **AIDA – Australian Institute of Dramatic Arts – International**
  www.AIDAacting.com **2002 – Ongoing**
  (Teaching online since April 2020)
  Founder, Artistic Director, Lecturer, Teacher, Coach

- **Performance Coaching with Paul Parker & Associates**
  www.paulparkerpc.com.au **2012 - Ongoing**
  Private and corporate business and presenter coaching on Skype and in person

- **TAFTA – Australia 2014–2020**
  Advanced master class acting teaching and ongoing 20- and 40-week course teaching across Melbourne, Adelaide, Sydney and Gold Coast

- **Stone Wings Acting School, Tokyo, Japan 2019**
- **Ascend Feather, Tokyo, Japan 2019**
- **AIDA Advanced Acting Classes USA 2019**
  Hollywood, Los Angeles and Manhattan, New York

- **Stone Wings Acting School, Tokyo, Japan 2018**
- **Ascend Feather, Tokyo, Japan 2018**
- **AIDA Advanced Acting Classes USA 2018**
  Hollywood, Los Angeles and Manhattan, New York

- **Mystique Productions Adelaide,** Australia **2017–18**
- **Jikei International, Tokyo and Osaka, Japan 2017**
- **Stawell Performing Arts Company, Australia 2017**
- **Stone Wings Acting School, Tokyo, Japan 2017**
- **Jikei International, Tokyo** and Osaka, Japan 2017
- **Ascend Feather, Tokyo, Japan 2017**
- **Film & Television Studio International – Australia 2016**

- **Stone Wings Acting School, Tokyo, Japan 2016**
- **Jikei International, Tokyo, Japan 2016**
- **Engeki Workshop, Tokyo, Japan 2016**
- **AIDA Advanced Acting Classes USA 2016**
  Hollywood, Los Angeles and Manhattan, New York
- **Ascend Feather, Tokyo, Japan 2016**
  Corporate business coaching on the presentation of self in business
- **RMIT University, Melbourne, Australia 2015**
  Coaching on self-presentation in business
- **Advanced Acting Classes, AIDA/Performance Coaching 2015 with Paul Parker & Associates in USA**
- **Stone Wings Acting School, Tokyo, Japan 2015**
  Advanced on camera and theatre acting classes
- **Ascend Feather, Tokyo, Japan 2015**
  Corporate business coaching on the presentation of self in business
- **Ararat Rural City 2014**
  Adjudicating the *One Act Theatre Play Festival* – Ararat, Victoria
- **AIDA Advanced Acting Classes USA 2014**
  Hollywood, Los Angeles & Manhattan, New York
- **Stone Wings Acting School, Tokyo Japan 2014**
  Advanced on camera and theatre acting classes.
- **Stone Wings Acting School, Tokyo Japan 2013**
  Australian acting and on camera technique teaching adults
- **Ascend Feather, Tokyo, Japan 2013**
  Teaching businessman on self-presentation and creativity and the use of their voice
- **Australian Institute of Dramatic Arts, AIDA, USA 2002–11**
  Artistic Director, Lecturer, Teacher, Coach, working with both

international and domestic students in Los Angeles, New York, Chicago, San Francisco. Adults and teenagers

- **International Performing Arts Conference 2006–2011 Los Angeles Center Studios, USA**

    Teaching a *conference opener* acting class. Industry audience of 2,500 + Adjudicator of actor competition held in various locations in Los Angeles and San Francisco, California, USA

- **Geely University, Beijing, China 2010**
    Teaching actors Australian acting method and on-camera technique

- **University Sanya College, Hainan Province, China 2010**
    Teaching actors Australian acting method and on-camera technique

- **Victorian Arts Centre, Art Education Program 1996** *Winterarts* **Melbourne, Victoria.** Contract Drama Coach for primary and secondary students in Victoria and in Albury in New South Wales

- **Holmesglen Institute of TAFE, Melbourne, Victoria 1996** (Tertiary and Further Education) Drama/Acting guest lecturer

- **Northern Melbourne Institute of TAFE Victoria 1995–96** Drama Teacher/Lecturer for Victorian Certificate of Education/year 12 (V.C.E.) Theatre Studies and Post–Secondary Education, Diploma of Arts for *Small Companies and Community Theatre* course

- **Australian College of Dramatic Arts, Victoria 1995**

- **The School of Mines and Industries Ballarat Limited 1994 TAFE Victoria.** Post-Secondary Education Lecturer/Teacher for Associate Diploma of Arts for *Small Companies and Community Theatre* course

- **Highvale Secondary College, Victoria 1992**
    Head, Drama Department

- The Victorian Centre for Youth Arts St. Martins Theatre Victoria 1990–91

Above: One of the posters advertising Paul's 2014 Japan teaching tour. One of the class pictures for the 2013 Tokyo workshop, is in inset on the lower right.

Full listing of Paul Parker's credits as a director

THEATRE

USA

- **AIDA Showcase** National tour of: Hollywood Los Angeles, **2009** Off Broadway – New York and San Francisco
- **AIDA Showcase** Hollywood – Los Angeles **2006**
- **AIDA Comedy Shows** Hollywood – Los Angeles **2006/2005** 11 shows over 2 years, including two at The Viper Room on the Sunset Strip in Los Angeles
- **AIDA Showcase** Hollywood – Los Angeles **2004**
- **AIDA Open Performance Days** Hollywood – L.A. **2004, 2006, 2009**

JAPAN

- ***Night*** *by Harold Pinter, Stone Wings Acting School,* **2015**, Tokyo, Japan.

Above: Paul directing SMB Drama students, performing simulated activations, at Sovereign Hill in Ballarat, Victoria, Australia, in 1994.

AUSTRALIA

- **Can You See The Sea** Stawell West Primary School, **2017**
- **Lady Windemere's Fan** Assistant Director: Melbourne Theatre Company, Melbourne **1995**
- **Ringside** Begonia Festival – Street Theatre, SMB Ballarat **1995**
- **Clean Up Australia Day** Street Theatre, SMB Ballarat **1994**
- **Walk Against Want** C.A.B. – Street Theatre, SMB Ballarat **1994**

Above: A newspaper article about Paul securing the deal for students to perform at Sovereign Hill. Sovereign Hill Deputy Director, museum services, Michael Evans and the head of the street theatre activations Gary Tobin are also in the picture from The Courier magazine in Ballarat in 1994.

- **Street Theatre Activations** Sovereign Hill Historical **1994** Park SMB Ballarat
- **Red Riding Hood** Highvale Secondary College **1992** Glen Waverley, Melbourne
- **Whose Home It?** Highvale Secondary College **1992** Glen Waverley, Melbourne
- **Whose Home Is It?** St. Martins The Victorian Centre **1991** for Youth Arts, South Yarra, Melbourne
- **The House Project** St. Martins The Victorian Centre. **1990** for Youth Arts, South Yarra, Melbourne

Above: Paul in the Playbill as Assistant Director of Lady Windermere's Fan at Melbourne Theatre Company in Australia in 1995.

VARIETY

- **Widdle & Piddle** (clowning) Director Ikea Showrooms, Schools, Street Theatre **1990–91**

FILM (all on IMDB)

- **I'm A Tradie** – Production **in 2022**
- **Where To From Here?** – Shot in Melbourne, Australia **2018**
- **Stewart's Annual Shearing** – Shot in Central Victoria, Australia **2018**
- **Die San Vacuum Cleaner** – Shot in Tokyo, Japan **2017**
- **Neighbours – a Drama** – Shot in Tokyo, Japan **2017**
- **Neighbours – a Comedy** – Shot in Tokyo, Japan **2017**
- **Rinse & Repeat** – Shot in Melbourne, Australia **2017**

PRE-PRODUCTION/SCRIPT DEVELOPMENT

- N.F. Feature film **2023?**

TELEVISION *(On IMDB)*

- **The Travel Counsellor. Television Series** (Supervising Director – Day one) **2019**

ACTORS VIDEO SHOW REELS

- Bianca Witts **2021**
- Hollie Kirby **2017**
- Casey Brimble **2017**
- Chris Erasmus **2016**
- Jack Antoniou **2016**
- Kyoko Kudo **2015**

FORMAL TRAINING

- **National Institute of Dramatic Art** (Winter Director's Program)
- **Deakin University/ Victoria College – Rusden** (Bachelor of Education)

Full Listing of Paul Parker's credits as an actor

International Awards

Best Actor – Winner in an **ENSEMBLE CAST** for **The Love Of Freedom** in NAACP Theatre Awards, Los Angeles, 2001.

Best Actor - Winner – of a heat **& Runner Up to best Actor** - of a heat, in a television role, where Paul was given a prize amount of money at Ballarat South St., Eisteddfod, Australia, 1998. Paul would like to stipulate that I did not win the overall competition and an immediate role on "Neighbours" television show. He had to audition for "Neighbours" at a later date, before he acted on the television show.

FILM

Feature films:

- ELOISE – Lead, Dannaher Productions. Dir: Brenden Dannaher
- LIFE AS A BLUE RINGED OCTOPUS – Co-Star, Rayon Productions Dir: Garnet Mae
- THE ELIXIR – Supporting, Pinnacle Movies Dir: Colm O'Murchu
- WINDTALKERS – Featured, M.G.M./Island Wind Productions Dir: John Woo

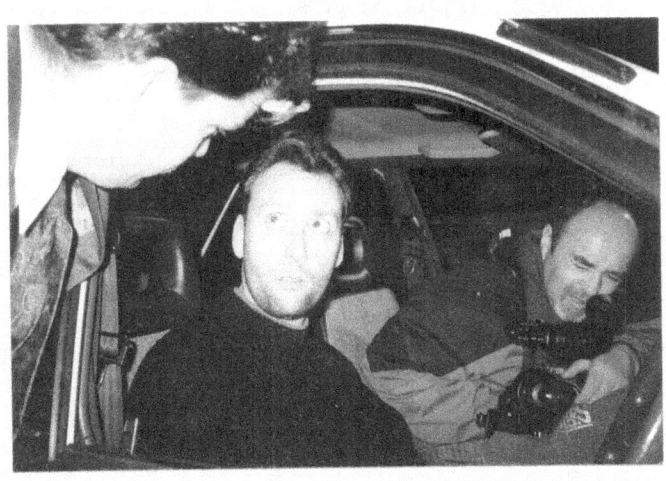

Above: Paul on set in the lead role of the film Murder To Go with actor Jason Buckley in 1996. Jason has 35 IMDB credits as of June, 2022. Director: Mark Hughes. Amazingly, Paul has performed professionally with Jason Buckley in film, television sketch comedy and theatre.

Short films:

- BOXES OF BOOKS: Co-Star, V.C.A. School of Film & T.V., Dir: Briony Kidd
- BRICK ISLAND: Lead, (USA) Dir: Steven Winarski
- BROKEN GLASS – Lead, Dir: Adam Daniel
- BRUISED – Co-Star, Dir: Emmanuelle Schick Garcia
- CARMEN'S FANTASY – Co-Star, Open Channel Short Film, Dir: Richard Veith
- CLEAN – Co-Star, V.C.A. School of Film & T.V., Dir: Jake Robb
- CREATURES OF HOLLYWOOD – (USA) Supporting, Tone Ent., Dir: Douglas Kennett
- EMILY & SARAH – Co-Star, Non Linear Pictures, Dir: David Manefield
- ETERNAL FLAME – Lead, Independent Film, Dir: Stuart Partridge
- FACELIFT – Lead, Independent Short Film, Dir: Jan Czajkowski
- GEORGE MEET EVAN – Lead, U.T.S. Production, Dir: Jane Lee Spicer
- INTERRUPTUS – Lead, Bug Bear Productions, Dir: Tonya Peppitt
- IN THE RED – Featured, Burnin' Bones Pty Ltd, Dir: Glenn Ruehland
- LAST 40 SHOTS OF JOHN BONHAM (USA) Supporting, Dir: Lance Whinery
- LOVE MONSTER – Lead, Open Channel Production, Dir: Mark Hughes
- MURDER TO GO – Lead, Independent Short Film, Dir: Mark Hughes
- RUBBER CHICKEN SOCIETY MOVIE (USA) – Co-Star, Dir: Jon Schnitzer
- SALESMANIAC – Co-star, Dir: Andrew Handelmann
- SIX O'CLOCK SWILL – Supporting, Liam Branagan Productions, Dir: Eve Spence

- SOLE WITNESS – Co-Star, Boathouse Productions, Dir: Brendan Danneher
- SOCIAL INSECURITY – Lead, Independent Short Film, Dir: Michael Cleland
- STEWARTS ANNUAL SHEARING – supporting, Player Productions
- THE SPRINT QUEEN -Co-Star, Open Channel, Dir: Stephen Hutchance
- THE PINK SLIP – Lead, P D's Productions, Dir: Pru Donovan
- THE VISITOR – Lead, Rusden Media Graduates Production
- THURSDAY – Seven Short Splinters – Co-Star Open Channel, Production, Dir: Anthony Snowden
- VAMPAGE – Co-Star V.C.A. School of Film & T.V., Dir: Blair Jackson
- WHERE TO FROM HERE? – supporting, Player Productions
- WITNESS – Featured, Dir: Monika Mitchell

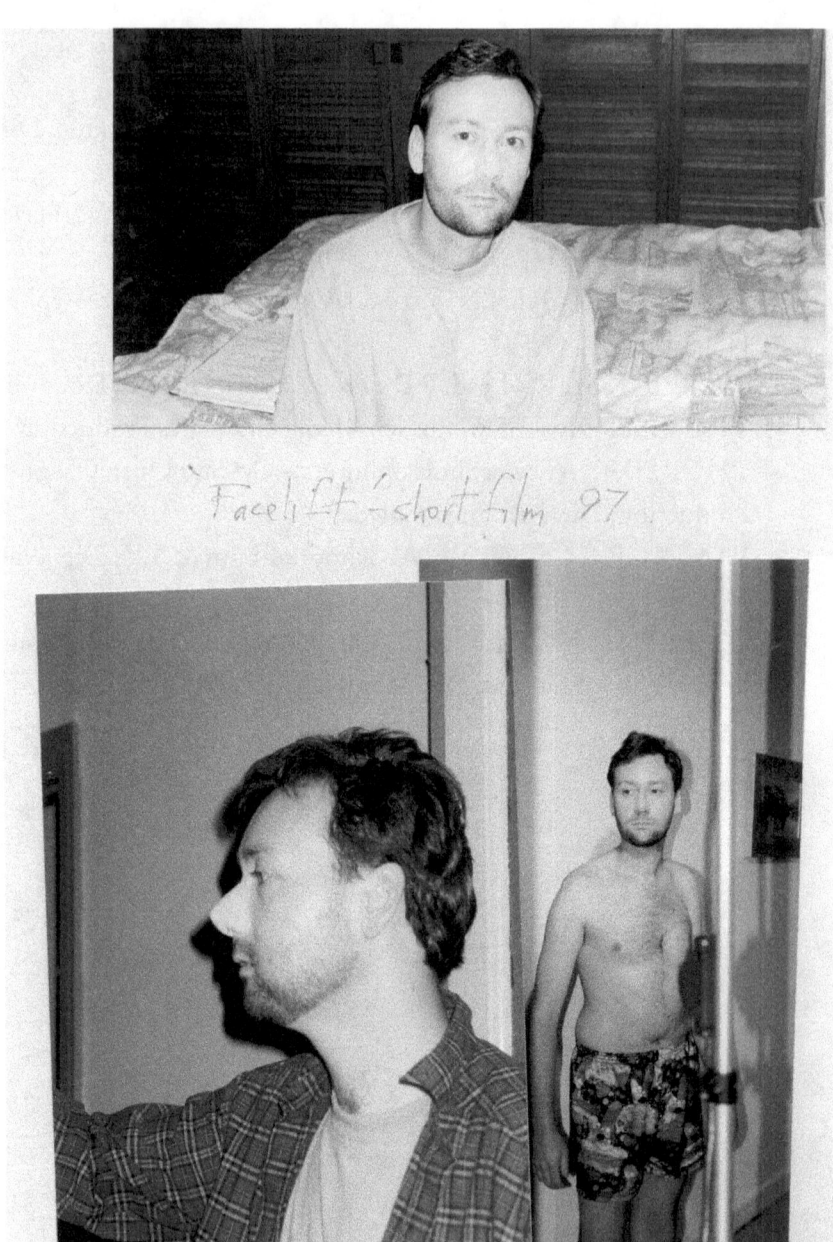

Above: Paul in the lead role of the short film Facelift. Directed by Polish director Jan Czajkowski in Melbourne in 1997. This film screened in London in England and in Warsaw in Poland.

Above: Some pictures from some more short films.
Top: on set in The Sprint Queen with actor Colin Donald in Melbourne in 1997.
Middle: Love Monster, 1997.
Above bottom: The Last 40 Shots of John Bonham in Los Angeles in 2002.

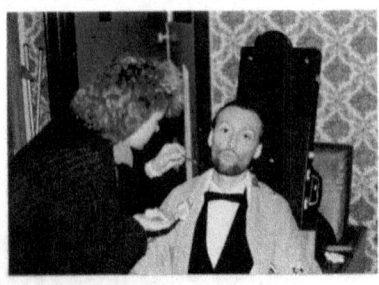

Above two top pics: Paul's first short film The Visitor with actor Greg Fleet in 1986 in Melbourne. (Paul was made up to look old).
Above middle: Sketch television: One Step, Two Step, Tickle Under There – where Paul played six characters in comedy sketches. Directed by Richard Hearman from Asylum Films.
Above bottom pic: Love Monster.

SIX O'CLOCK SWILL

A short film by
EVE SPENCE

Above: Paul in the short film Six O'clock Swill. This time with Jason Clarke (72 IMDB credits), John McNeil (41 IMDB credits) and Annie Bryon (43 IMDB credits) as of June, 2022. The film was shot in Sydney. Cast by Mullinars Casting. 2000.

TELEVISION

- A.M. ADELAIDE – Lead, Life – What A Front! H.S.V. 7 Adelaide.
- AUSTRALIA'S MOST WANTED – Co-Star, Grundy TV, Dir: David Morgan
- FULL FRONTAL – Many sketches – Two Episodes Artist Services, Dir: Ted Emery
- FUNKY SQUAD – Featured, Working Dog Pty Ltd, Dir: Jane Kennedy
- IN ALL YOUR GLORY – Co-Star, Channel 7. Promo to the 2000 Olympic Games in Sydney. Artist Services.
- NEIGHBOURS – Co-Star, Grundy TV, Dir: Jovita O'Shaughnessy
- ONE STEP, TWO STEP, TICKLE UNDER – Lead, Asylum Films, Dir: Richard Hearman
- PLAY OF THE MOMENT (Pilot) USA – Series Regular, Channel 10 Adelphia, Dir: Marcia Singer
- PHANTOM MUGGER (Pilot) USA – Series Regular Dir: Remus Dabb
- THAT'S ALMOST ENTERTAINING – Co-Star, Syndicated Comedy Productions
- THE REAPER (Sitcom Pilot) – Co-Star, Anything But Productions
- THE SULLIVANS – ongoing featured/Supporting, Dir: Pino Amenta, Lex Van Os & others
- WILD ASS OF A MAN – Featured – ABC TV
- THE YOUNG AND THE RESTLESS – USA – Day Player – Ian Haskell CBS TV, Dir: Sally McDonald

Pictured above: Paul on the CBS lot, about to go on set as an actor, on the Young and The Restless television show in Los Angeles in 2003.

TELEVISION COMMERCIALS

- DARK MOMENTS – GUINNESS – Lead, A.P.A. Director: Sonja Heller 100% 30sec.
- DIGILINE EDITING SUITES – Lead, Dir: Stuart Partridge – Lead, Role – 100% 15 sec.
- LION RED – Lead Blue Sky Pictures, Dir: Jason Wingrove 100% 45sec

THEATRE

- "2 B or Not 2 B @ 2033": Role of Hamlet. An adaptation of Hamlet – Prince Of Denmark by William Shakespeare. Directed by Tony Armatrading from the Royal Shakespeare Company/ National Theatre. Cast included: James Avery, Brad Blaisdell,

Alex Peabody Julius Noflin and James Armstrong, Los Angeles, USA
- BACK & BEYOND: Brandon Cooke – Lead Gasworks Theatre, Dir: Lyndal Marguerite
- CRIME SCENE: Rockalypse Now Chef – Co-Star Sacred Fools Theatre, Dir: Dean Cameron. USA
- FISH OUT OF WATER: Beaver – Lead ensemble – Collingwood Children's Farm, Victoria, Australia, Dir: Kimberley Evans
- FOR THE LOVE OF FREEDOM: Sonthonax – Costar Greenway / Robey Theatre Co., Dir: Ben Guillory. Los Angeles, USA

Above: Paul playing the beaver in Fish Out of Water at Collingwood Children's Farm in the 1990s. Pictured below: Paul as Sonthonax in For The Love of Freedom at Greenway Court Theatre in Los Angeles in 2001.

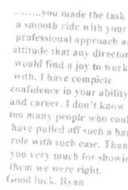

Above: Paul in the staged play Fur Better Or Worse at Gasworks Theatre.

- FUR BETTER OR WORSE: Tony/Felix – Lead, Gasworks Theatre, Dir: Ryan Letch
- GET A LIFE!: Frank lead, La Mama Theatre, Dir: Ella Filar
- IMPRO DOT COMEDY: Main Ensemble Stables Theatre
- KING LEAR: Burgundy/Messenger – Co-Star Australian Shakespeare Co., Dir: N. Warrington
- LIFE – WHAT A FRONT!: Matthew – Lead 11th Int'l Comedy Festival, Dir: Steve Wheat
- LIFE – WHAT A FRONT!: Matthew – Lead – Adelaide Fringe Festival, Dir: Jackie Kennedy

- LISTEN TO ME: Jimmy – Lead, Gasworks Theatre, Dir: Jocene Vallack

- PRINCESS & THE PIG FARMER: Brian – Co-Star, Gasworks Theatre, Dir: Paul Wentford
- STILL LIFE: Marty – Lead, Gasworks Theatre, Dir: Jacqui Kennedy
- THE FIRST WOMAN: Charles – Co-Star, Lankershim Arts Centre, Dir: Ayana Cahrr
- THEATERSPORTS: main Ensemble, St. Martins Theatre/Playhouse Arts Centre
- TRANSLATIONS: Hugh – Lead, St. Martins Theatre, Dir: Briony Dunn

Above: Paul in two media articles on the play Translations, written by Brian Friel.

COLLEGE & COMMUNITY THEATRE

- (scenes from) The Dumb Waiter – Gus – Lead, Victoria College – Rusden
- (scenes from) The Zoo Story – Jerry – Lead, Victoria College – Rusden
- (scenes from) The Homecoming – Lenny – Lead, Victoria College – Rusden
- (scenes from) Curse of the Starving Class – Wesley – Lead, Victoria College Rusden
- (scenes from) Amadeus Mozart – Lead, Victoria College – Rusden
- Numerous – Main Ensemble Victoria College – Rusden
- Next Page Please – Billy – Lead, Victoria College – Rusden
- Much Ado About Nothing – Don Pedro – Supporting, Victoria College – Rusden
- Romeo & Juliet Benvolio – Supporting, Box Hill College theatre
- He Who Says Yes and No – Teacher – Lead, Box Hill College theatre
- Ringside – Various – Lead, Begonia Festival, Ballarat
- Madwoman of Chaillot – Broker – Supporting, Heidelberg Theatre Company
- Habeas Corpus – Mr. Purdue – Supporting, Heidelberg Theatre Company
- Royal Hunt of the Sun – Diego – Supporting, Heidelberg Theatre Company
- Lion in Winter – Phillip II – Supporting, Heidelberg Theatre Company
- Lloyd George Knew My Father – Simon – Supporting, Heidelberg Theatre Company
- The Gingerbread Lady – Manuel – Supporting, Heidelberg Theatre Company
- The Play's the Thing – Dwornitschek – Supporting, Heidelberg Theatre Company

Above: Paul's first theatre performance out of high school in 1979. Playing Johann Dwornitschek in Ferenc Molnar's play The Play's the Thing at Heidelberg Theatre Company in Melbourne.

STAND-UP COMEDY: 1977 to 1990

All in Victoria, Australia.

- Elbow Greese at Jed's in Nicholson St, Carlton
- Armadale Hotel
- Star & Garter
- Espy Comedy at the Esplanade in St. Kilda
- Compere, Armadale Hotel – Variety Night
- Theatresports, St. Martins Theatre/Playhouse
- Le Joke, Last Laugh Comedy Theatre
- Variety Nights in Arthurs Creek, Hurstbridge, St. Andrews, Panton Hill, Whittlesea, Heidelberg

CLOWNING

Widdle & Piddle clowning duet with Julienne Verhagen and clowning also with Ngaire Henderson. Performances included busking, corporate companies, schools, markets, etc.

Below: Over the years Paul has received dozens of reference letters on his acting ability and success. Here is just one of them, from the USA.

November, 1, 2001

TO WHOM IT MAY CONCERN

I am pleased to write this reference for Paul Parker. I came across Paul at the auditions for our theatre companies production of "For The Love of Freedom" a trilogy by Levy Lee Simon. Paul performed a monologue from the character Biff from Death of A Salesman by Arthur Miller at the first auditions. I was so impressed by Paul's performance that I called him back where he read for many characters that demonstrated his exceptional range and ability. Paul was ultimately cast in the role of Sonthonax in the production that ran in June, July of 2001 at the Greenway Court Theatre on Fairfax in Los Angeles.

During rehearsals I realized Paul's preparation and diligence produced a performance revelation. He is an actor of outstanding ability. He improvised constantly within the confines of the text and worked exceptionally well with fellow actors while on stage that constantly produced different results. In addition he took my direction immediately and was a delight to direct. Paul is also a very intelligent actor who constantly develops his characters, what is going on in the scene, what he wants and then pushes their boundaries. I concluded that Paul would be an asset to the ongoing development of the trilogy, indeed he would be an asset to any ensemble.

Paul's performance in the production was outstanding. He received constant positive comments from the Producers of the production; fellow cast members, theatre critics and the public at large. His work produced a standard of excellence that reverberated through the ensemble.

One theatre critic, Don Grigware, from the theatre section of the Valley Scene described his performance saying: "P.J. Parker was the standout as the evil Sonthonax" in the production. No mean feets as the entire cast won an acting award as "Best Ensemble Cast" at the NAACP Theatre Awards held at the Directors Guild in Los Angeles in November 2001. "For the Love of Freedom" was nominated for a total of ten (10) NAACP Image Theatre Awards.

The Robey Theatre Company is looking forward to working with Paul again.

Yours sincerely,

Ben Guillory
Artistic Director
Robey Theatre Company

My second book:

ACTING FOR THE SCREEN

PAUL PARKER (B.ED.)
INTERNATIONAL ACTING TEACHER/ACTING COACH

TOPICS:

- Act On Camera
- Australian acting training for USA actors
- Differences between Australian and USA actor training
- Create Characters
- Scene Study
- Movement
- Role Playing
- Teaching Japanese actors

...And much, much more. The book should be available to purchase in 2023.